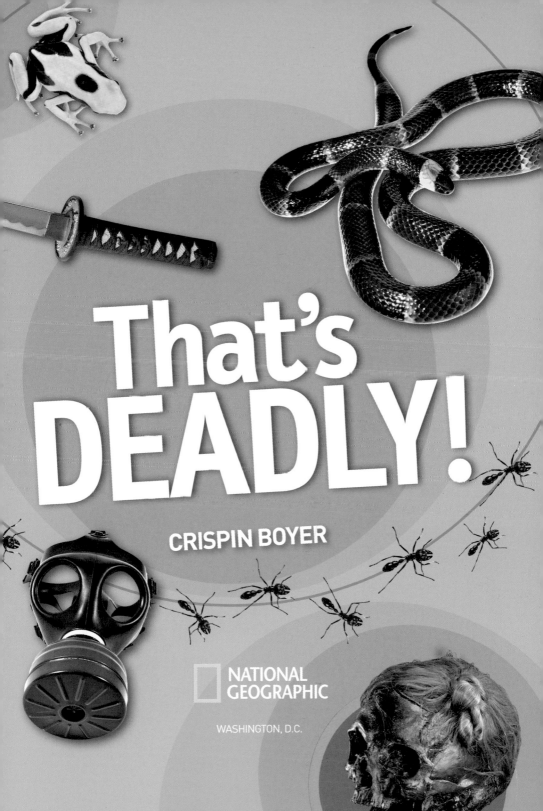

That's DEADLY!

CRISPIN BOYER

![NATIONAL GEOGRAPHIC] NATIONAL GEOGRAPHIC

WASHINGTON, D.C.

DEADLY Contents

Meet Your **Deadly** Host!

Meet Your Deadly Host!

ABANDON HOPE, ALL YE WHO OPEN THIS BOOK. CERTAIN DEATH AWAITS! Prepare to ponder pages of perilous plagues, doomsday disasters, and venomous predators with pointy teeth! Lurking in the margins: me, the Grim Reaper—the embodiment of death across many cultures—watching and waiting to claim the next poor sap poised at the finish line of life. My, don't you look like the picture of health today. No matter. I've got all the time in the world. *Muahahaha!*

Ahem. Sorry for the scary spiel. I was just trying to get your attention. Timothy's my name, and grim-reaping is my game. Yep, death is a heck of a way to make a living, but I can't complain. Good dental benefits. (Pearly whites are important when you lack lips.) I get to carry this cool scythe (loaded with apps and a built-in Wi-Fi hot spot, of course). But portraying the deity of doom is strictly a nine-to-five gig. When the bell tolls at quitting time, I drop the gloomy act and let my hair down. (Well, figuratively speaking.)

But whether I'm stalking the soon-to-be deceased or coaching my nephew's T-ball team (go T-Bones!), I'm always the biggest expert on expiration in the room. I figure that makes me the perfect MC for everything deadly!

Now, I wasn't kidding when I said this book has some scary stuff, but it's not all doomsday scenarios and animals with awesome jaws. You'll also unearth tales of terminating toys and killer careers, stories of bloody sports and meat-eating plants, firsthand accounts of lightning strikes and harmful hobbies. By the time you finish *That's Deadly!*, you'll know how to survive a shark attack, where to find (and avoid) the world's most dangerous cow, and who would win in a tussle between a ninja and a pirate. Look for me along the way when you want some bonus fatal facts. Until then, I've got work to do ...

TIM THE GRIM REAPER

How to Get the Most From

That's DEADLY!

STEP 1: WATCH OUT!

As you journey through *That's Deadly!*, keep an eye peeled for these fatal features ...

FATAL FACTS: Tim the Grim Reaper's centuries of service as the Angel of Death has made him the ultimate expert on terminal topics. Watch for your cloaked host to surface from the shadows and share bonus bits of deadly data.

OPPOSITES ATTACK: Occasionally we'll pit two vastly different topics against each other in a duel to see which is more deadly.

SURVIVORS' STORIES: Look for interviews with people who have faced death and lived to tell the tale.

STEP 2: KNOW YOUR TERMINAL TERMINOLOGY!

This book is full of terms that rarely pop up in your everyday life. If you're ever stumped by the meaning of a word, flip back to this glossary for a fast refresher.

ANTIVENOM: Medicine that can counteract the deadly effects of snake and insect venom.

AVALANCHE: A fast flow of snow down a mountainside.

WARNING:

This book contains deadly dilemmas, wild weather, scary situations, and spine-chilling species that you want to stay far away from. While National Geographic works hard to ensure all information for surviving and avoiding these things is accurate and up to date, always exercise caution. In other words, when it comes to anything dangerous or risky: Don't Do It!

BASE JUMPING: A type of low-altitude skydiving from fixed objects.

CATACLYSM: A massive and violent event that brings change. A catastrophe.

EXTINCTION: The death of an entire species.

GERMS: Infectious microscopic bacteria, viruses, and parasites that make humans sick.

HOLD-DOWN: A dangerous dip into deep water propelled by the force of a crashing wave.

INFECTIOUS: Able to pass from person to person.

PANDEMIC: An outbreak of a deadly disease that spreads across a country or the world.

POISON: A substance that causes sickness or even death when inhaled, swallowed, or absorbed.

RIP CORD: The cord that triggers the release of a parachute while skydiving.

SACRIFICE: A ritual offering to please a god or other higher power.

TOXIN: A poison or venom produced by a plant or animal.

TSUNAMI: An destructive wave caused by earthquakes and undersea avalanches.

VENOM: A toxic substance created by animals for offense or defense.

VENOMOUS: A type of animal capable of transmitting poison through bites or stings. These animals inject their venom into victims.

STEP 3: GET READY TO RATE!

As part of his job as the all-powerful Angel of Death, Tim the Grim Reaper developed the Kill-o-Meter to measure degrees of deadliness. The higher he ranks something on the scale, the deadlier it is! You'll find these ratings at the end of each chapter. If you disagree with them, make your own Kill-o-Meter scale and poll your pals!

SUDDEN DEATH

RUN FOR YOUR LIFE!

DANGER ZONE

RISKY BUSINESS

CROSSING THE STREET
1 IN 723 CHANCE

ODDS OF ENDS

CHOKING ON FOOD
1 IN 3,649 CHANCE

AT TIMES, THIS BOOK MAY HAVE YOU CONVINCED THAT EVERYTHING IS OUT TO KILL YOU. NOT TRUE! IF AT ANY TIME YOU BECOME OVERWHELMED BY ALL THE GLOOM AND DOOM IN THESE PAGES, FLIP BACK HERE AND CONSIDER YOUR RELATIVELY LOW RISK OF DYING FROM THE FOLLOWING STRANGE CIRCUMSTANCES ...

AIR AND SPACE ACCIDENT
1 IN 8,357 CHANCE

HORNET, WASP, OR BEE STING
1 IN 75,852 CHANCE

CATACLYSMIC STORM
1 IN 83,922 CHANCE

FALLING VENDING MACHINE

1 IN 112 MILLION CHANCE

LIGHTNING STRIKE

1 IN 136,011 CHANCE

FALLING COCONUT

1 IN 41.1 MILLION CHANCE

FIREWORKS ACCIDENT

1 IN 340,733 CHANCE

SHARK ATTACK

1 IN 3.7 MILLION CHANCE

* All statistics are for the United States only, except for shark attacks and falling coconuts, which are global figures.

CHAPTER 1

The Bad Ol' Days

PLAGUES, PIRATES, PISTOL DUELS, APOCALYPTIC DISASTERS—the darkest days of our past can turn history class into a horror movie. And in this chapter, it's showtime! Prepare to dive into the deadliest decades of humanity's history, from pestilence to pistol duels, super soldiers to ancient murders. Survive to the end of this chapter and you'll hope that history never, ever repeats itself.

Outbreak!

The Black Death ravaged medieval Europe ...

WEAKENED BY WARS AND FAILED CROPS, ENGLAND IN A.D. 1347 WAS A ROTTEN PLACE TO LIVE FOR HUMANS, BUT IT WAS PARADISE FOR GERMS: those icky bacteria, viruses, and parasites that make humans sick. England's crowded, filthy, rat-infested cities were especially fertile territories for an infectious rod-shaped bacteria barely a hundredth of the size of a flea. Today, scientists call the bacteria *Yersinia pestis,* but it is better known as the bubonic plague or, simply, the Black Death. It killed one in three people in Europe at the time—it lived up to its name.

The bubonic plague is one of history's first pandemics: infectious diseases that spread quickly across countries, continents, or even the world. The plague became known as the Black Death for its fearsome symptoms. Victims developed dark and painful egg-size lumps called buboes in their armpits and other sensitive areas. The disease only got worse from there (you don't really want to know the later symptoms), until the victim fell into a coma and perished. Variations of the plague were even deadlier. Spread through coughs and sneezes, pneumonic plague infected the lungs. The septicemic plague infected the blood. Everyone who caught it was a goner.

Doctors today have a cure for the Black Death, but people in 14th-century Europe didn't know about bacteria or understand how diseases spread. They believed the plague was a punishment from the heavens, or it was caused by stinky odors in the air (which is why many Europeans wore perfume or clutched flowers to their noses). Actually, the plague started in China, where it was carried by fleas that traveled on rats. The rats stowed away on trading ships that sailed to ports of call throughout Europe. Once these rodents reached villages and cities, the fleas pounced onto people, biting them and quickly spreading the infection. Fearful residents took to living in the sewers to avoid the plague (it didn't work).

Plague treatments ranged from dangerous to ridiculous. Victims ate

MORE **DEADLY** DISEASES ...

FLU PANDEMIC

- A flu pandemic in 1918 killed as many as 100 million people around the world (the virus used to be more serious than it is today).

- The Spanish conquest of the New World in the 15th century spread smallpox, a highly contagious disease that killed more than a third of the Native American population. In the 20th century, smallpox was responsible for more than 300 million deaths until vaccinations wiped out the viruses responsible for the disease.

- Until doctors developed a vaccine that wiped it out in the 1950s, polio was a terrifying disease that could cause paralysis and death.

POLIO

SMALLPOX

ground-up emeralds or washed themselves in urine or rubbed their buboes with a chicken's plucked rear end. None of those remedies worked, of course. If a medieval doctor used a hot poker to burst the puss- and blood-filled buboes, the patient might pull through. This treatment became more common during an outbreak in 1361, but it wasn't enough to stop the plague from ravaging Europe several more times right up to the mid-19th century. One out of every six people in London died from the Black Death in 1665 alone. Until medical science invented antibiotic medicine to battle the plague bacteria, the only surefire cure was isolation. Infected families would lock their doors and mark them with black crosses, often along with the message "Lord have mercy on us."

TIM
THE GRIM REAPER'S
FATAL FACTS

One of the worst careers in 17th-century London was the "searcher of the dead," who had the grim job of going door-to-door and carting away victims of the plague. Talk about a dead-end job!

COLD CASE
AN ANCIENT MURDER

HE MIGHT HAVE SKIN LIKE BEEF JERKY AND A FACE ONLY A ZOMBIE'S MOTHER WOULD LOVE, BUT ÖTZI THE ICEMAN STILL LOOKS FANTASTIC FOR HIS AGE. Two German hikers found his withered body facedown high in the Ötztal Alps along the Austrian-Italian border in 1991. Thinking they had discovered the victim of a recent mountain-climbing accident, the hikers called the authorities. It turns out Ötzi's death was neither recent nor an accident. He had been murdered more than 5,000 years ago. The hikers had stumbled on a crime scene from the Copper Age.

Freeze-dried by the frigid, arid air of the Alpine region where he died (and nicknamed for it), Ötzi is the world's oldest natural mummy. Perfectly preserved specimens of ancient corpses are extremely rare, making Ötzi a scientific treasure. By studying his body, archaeologists can learn about life in an age when simple metal tools were still state of the art and hunting was the only way to make a living. After prodding and x-raying Ötzi's heavily tattooed body, scientists unearthed a trove of information. They know what he ate for his last meal (grains and some roasted goat). They know that he died in the spring or summer. They know he was in his mid-40s—a ripe old age in his dangerous time. And they know he suffered from many health ailments, from bad teeth to sore joints to parasitic worms that likely left him with a constant upset stomach. He carried with him essential tools, including a bow and arrows and a primitive first-aid kit, for survival in the Alpine wilderness.

The scientists also learned how Ötzi died. Scans of his body revealed a stone arrowhead buried in his left shoulder. He'd been shot in the back! Dizzy from blood loss, Ötzi the Iceman fell to the ground in a desolate pass known as Tisenjoch. A fracture on the back of his skull shows either that he hit his head or that someone delivered the final blow before the Iceman had a chance to bleed to death.

The one mystery scientists can't solve is this: Who killed the Iceman? Clues from the crime scene help reconstruct the drama that unfolded at 6,500 feet (2,000 m). An injury to Ötzi's hand hints that he may have gotten in a recent scrap. He also carried a finely crafted copper axe, evidence that he was a high-ranking member of his tribe. Perhaps Ötzi had scuffled with rivals for his power in the days before his death, injuring his hand in the process. His trek up the mountain might have been an attempt to escape. We know today he didn't make it. More than five millennia later, Ötzi's body can tell us how he lived and died, but the identity of his killers remains lost to the mists of time.

TWO ANCIENT MURDER MYSTERIES ... **SOLVED**

KING TUT
DATE OF DEATH: 1323 B.C.
KILLED BY: INFECTION
King Tutankhamen, aka King Tut, wasn't the first boy king to rule ancient Egypt, but he is the most famous thanks to the discovery of his tomb and its trove of treasures in 1922. Archaeologists cut Tut into pieces to pry his body from the sticky sacred oils that coated the inside of his coffin, and such rough handling inflicted injuries on the 3,300-year-old mummy that made it tough to tell what really caused Tut's demise. Some suspected he was murdered. But modern technologies like 3-D scanning revealed that the all-powerful king was actually in poor health and had suffered a broken leg. Perhaps the frail pharaoh tumbled from one of the chariots found in his tomb. With his immune system already weakened, Tut could have easily died from an infection in the busted bone.

NEANDERTHAL MAN
DATE OF DEATH: 50,000 B.C.
KILLED BY: YOUR ANCESTOR
Between 50,000 and 70,000 years ago in what is now Iraq, a 40-something Neanderthal man in poor health was killed by a spear thrown into his chest. Close relatives of humans, Neanderthals died out about 20,000 years ago—possibly because humans bred them out of existence or hunted them to extinction. Studies of this Neanderthal's body (recovered from a cave in the 1950s) showed he was murdered. His killer was a human being; the evidence is the murder weapon itself. Only humans had learned how to wield a throwing spear. In the face of such advanced weapons technology, the poor Neanderthal man didn't stand a chance.

ARMED AND DANGEROUS

FIVE OF HISTORY'S MOST **FEARSOME** WARRIORS ...

SPARTAN SOLDIERS

TOUR OF DUTY: ANCIENT GREECE FROM THE 6TH TO THE 4TH CENTURY B.C.
WEAPONS OF CHOICE: SWORDS, SPEARS, AND LARGE BRONZE SHIELDS CALLED *HOPLONS*

The soldiers of Sparta were among the most feared warriors in history for a reason: Every man in this city-state (a city that's like its own country) was trained for battle since birth. Spartan babies had to pass an inspection for imperfections and weaknesses. At age 7, they were enrolled into a brutal military school called the *agoge*. It was like the world's worst summer camp—one that lasted year-round. Here they were barely fed, forced to sleep outside, and trained to wield weapons and fight.

Any boys who couldn't handle life in the agoge grew up to be second-class citizens. Graduates joined the army at age 20 and defended the city-state for life. Spartans fought in a fearsome formation called a phalanx. The warriors stood shoulder-to-shoulder several men deep, linking their shields to form a moving wall of metal and flicking spear points. Using this tactic, 300 Spartans held off hundreds of thousands of Persian invaders. It's no wonder the Spartans considered themselves descendents of Hercules, the buff hero of Greek mythology.

TIM THE GRIM REAPER'S FATAL FACTS | Spartans wore tunics the color of blood to hide their injuries from enemies in battle.

VIKINGS

TOUR OF DUTY: NORTHERN EUROPE AND NORTH AMERICA FROM A.D. 800 TO 1100
WEAPONS OF CHOICE: LONGBOATS, SWORDS, AND AXES

They came from the lands of ice and snow— the Scandinavian countries of northern Europe—to plunder the settlements of Britain, Ireland, and France. In fact, the name Viking means "a pirate raid" in the language of Old Norse. Expert sailors and boatbuilders, Vikings cruised up rivers in special flat-bottomed vessels to raid villages far from the sea. Before war, they prayed to Thor,

the god of thunder, and his trickster brother Loki. But while Vikings were terrifying warriors (some even donned wolf skins and howled in battle to fill their foes with dread), they could also be peaceful settlers, traders, and expert explorers. Five hundred years before Columbus set sail, a Viking named Leif Eriksson sailed from Greenland to "Vinland," now believed to be the northern tip of Newfoundland, Canada. Archaeologists in 1960 found evidence of Eriksson's settlement.

MEDIEVAL KNIGHTS

TOUR OF DUTY: EUROPE IN THE MIDDLE AGES (12TH TO 15TH CENTURY)
WEAPONS OF CHOICE: SWORDS, LANCES, WARHORSES, AND SUITS OF ARMOR THAT WEIGHED UP TO 50 POUNDS (23 KG)

These professional soldiers in shining armor were charged with protecting their lord's land from invaders, leading the castle's men-at-arms during sieges, and fighting on behalf of the church. Between battles, they competed in deadly games called tournaments to sharpen their skills. Armor, weapons, and warhorses cost more than a typical peasant might earn in a lifetime, so knights often hailed from noble families. The road to knighthood was long and rough. It started with a childhood full of boring chores and dangerous games. It ended at age 21 with a ceremonial smack to the head that knocked some men on their tails.

Along with a mastery of weapons and combat from a horse's saddle, knights were expected to act with chivalry: be generous and humble, protect the old and the weak, treat women with respect, and serve the church. In exchange for outstanding military service, they were granted their own lands—along with peasants to farm it—and noble titles. Successful knights found fortune and glory.

ENGLISH LONGBOWMEN

TOUR OF DUTY: GREAT BRITAIN AND FRANCE FROM THE 12TH TO THE 15TH CENTURY
WEAPONS OF CHOICE: WOODEN BOWS UP TO SIX FEET (1.8 M) LONG

Thunk! Thunk! Thunk! The most terrifying sound on the 13th-century battlefield wasn't the thundering charge of a knight's warhorse or the clang of sword striking shield. It was the impact of arrows, falling in torrents of sharpened-steel tips, as they pierced armor and the men who wore it. The bow was already an ancient weapon by the Middle Ages, but warriors in Wales invented a souped-up version that could launch arrows farther—up to 250 yards (229 m)—and with enough force to pierce solid oak. Each bow was made from a type of wood called yew, which became scarce in England after so many trees were felled to supply the military.

England's long-range archers were recruited from the ranks of commoners. They struck fear into the hearts of wealthy knights and changed the course of warfare. In one famous 1346 battle, 6,000 English longbowmen killed or injured 30,000 of France's finest soldiers. Pulling back the string of a longbow required almost super-human strength. Archers practiced for years, working their way up to the weapon. They were even forbidden from participating in any other sports on Sundays except for archery. Elite longbowmen could fire 20 arrows a minute into the ranks of charging knights, unhorsing them with each *thunk, thunk, thunk.*

SAMURAI

TOUR OF DUTY: FEUDAL JAPAN (12TH TO 18TH CENTURY)
WEAPONS OF CHOICE: KATANA SWORDS, BOWS, ORNATE BODY ARMOR, AND RIFLES

Similar to medieval knights, these Japanese warriors came from noble families, swore allegiance to powerful warlords, and trained from an early age to wield razor-sharp swords while wearing armor. But that's where the similarities ended. Samurai armor was built for flexibility rather than strength. It allowed these warriors to unleash sword attacks in a graceful blur rather than the brutal bashing delivered by medieval knights.

Samurai also followed a code—called the Bushido (or the way of the warrior)—that demanded bravery, honor, and obedience. And while the Bushido way might sound similar to the knight's chivalrous code, samurai were willing to pay the ultimate price if they failed in battle. Captured samurai vowed to take their own lives rather than bring dishonor on their families or their warlord.

OPPOSITES ATTACK

NINJAS VS.

A CENTURY SPANS THE RESPECTIVE GOLDEN AGES OF JAPAN'S NINJA WARRIORS AND THE CARIBBEAN'S MENACING PIRATES. But just because these fearsome fighters never met in combat doesn't mean we can't wonder at the outcome of their encounter. Brace yourselves for a battle of silence versus violence.

NINJAS

These black-clad warriors emerged from the shadows in the 16th century, when hundreds of power-hungry warlords squabbled over control of Japan. During this violent "feudal" era, warlords relied on their armies of noble samurai to defend their lands and attack rivals. But when they needed to fight dirty, the warlords hired ninjas for spying and assassination missions.

With no code of honor to put a damper on their business, ninjas hired themselves out to the highest bidder. A ninja on a mission needed to blend in anywhere, from a bustling village to a castle rooftop at midnight. That meant he or she (yes, some ninjas were women) was a master of disguise. When they weren't wearing their traditional full-body suit to blend in with the moonlight, ninjas would dress as farmers, merchants, or musicians to slip unnoticed through the countryside. The roots of the ninja stretch back to the eighth century—to secretive mountain clans trained in survival, self-defense, stealth, and evasion. Like all men and women who entered this dark trade, ninjas were feared and despised for their sneaky tactics and supposed supernatural powers. According to legend, ninjas could fly, walk on water, and vanish. Only one of these feats was false.

WICKED WEAPONRY

Ninja weapons were often modeled after the arsenal of the noble samurai, except adapted for a darker purpose. The ninja sword, called a ninjato, was similar to a samurai's blade but shorter, which made it easier to swing in cramped quarters and left room in the scabbard to stash blinding powder that could be flung at an enemy's eyes. Most ninja weaponry had multiple uses. The kusari-gama was a short bamboo pole with a sickle on one end and a long weighted chain on the other. It worked as a weapon (the chain swept enemies off their feet) or as a tool for climbing. Blade-tipped metal disks known as shuriken were used only to slow pursuers. Wouldn't you think twice about chasing a ninja if he or she started chucking razor-tipped stars in your direction?

PiRATES

Yo-ho, yo-ho—uh-oh! The sight of a mysterious ship flying a black flag on the horizon put a lump in the throats of 17th-century merchant sailors. That flag meant one thing: pirates! Faced with being chased by the faster, cannon-crammed vessels typically crewed by buccaneers, a merchant captain was left with two choices: lower the sails and surrender or turn and fight—and probably die.

PiRATES

The Pirates of the Caribbean movies portray buccaneer crews as likable bands of high-seas misfits, but real-life "freebooters" were ruthless thieves who relied on their cutthroat reputation to frighten ships into surrendering without a fight. After all, a ship plundered in one piece was worth more than a cannonball-riddled wreck. But if merchant ships didn't back down, pirates made good on their threat. They attacked with cannons to disable their victims' ship before boarding. Furious battles above- and belowdecks ensued, with the pirates wielding swords, pistols, and grenades. Merchants who fought back were given no quarter. Those who surrendered were invited to join the pirate crew ... or die.

Many pirates during the golden age of piracy (from the late 1600s to the early 1700s) were castoffs from the British and French navies. Unlike aboard navy vessels, pirate crews shared equally in the plunder and could vote in a new captain at any time should the current one fail to deliver. Still, life for the buccaneers was far from one swashbuckling adventure after another. Lousy food, cramped quarters, stinky crewmates, hurricanes, and terrifying sea battles were all part of the job.

NOT-SO-JOLLY ROGERS

No one knows who flew the first pirate flag, also known as the Jolly Roger. It was most likely a simple red or black strip of cloth hoisted above the ship's tallest mast to send a clear message to merchant ships: "Surrender or we'll sink you." Pirates during the golden age of piracy (from the late 1600s to the early 1700s) adorned their flags with skeletons, cutlasses, skulls and crossbones, drops of blood, and other scary symbols to instill as much fear as possible, turning their flags into weapons of psychological warfare.

WHICH IS MORE DEADLY?
NiNJAS!

While both pirates and ninjas were ruthless fighters, most pirates were little more than trained sailors or rescued slaves pressed into a career of high-seas robbery. They relied on their fearsome reputation rather than superior fighting skills to frighten victims into surrendering. Ninjas, on the other hand, were highly trained assassins and masters of martial arts and razor-sharp weaponry. A ninja clan would make short work of any buccaneer band they met on dry land.

BLOOD SPORTS

Four of History's Deadliest Games

CAMPBALL

If you think modern rugby and American football are brutal pastimes, you should've seen the game that inspired them. Called campball and played in England as far back as the 15th century, it was more of an all-out brawl rather than a game. Two teams tried to get an object—a shoe, a hat, an inflated pig bladder that served as a ball—from one end of town to the other using any means except fair play or sportsmanship. Chaos reigned, and games often ended with players beaten and bloodied. Nine players reportedly died of their injuries in one 19th-century game (remember, this was before the invention of helmets, pads, and other safety gear). Eventually, rules took hold and games became more structured, but it was always a dangerous sport.

GLADIATOR GAMES

More than 50,000 spectators gathered in Rome's Coliseum in the second century A.D. to witness gory spectacles: reenactments of famous battles, live hunts for exotic animals (released from cages kept in elaborate chambers under the sandy floor), and bloody battles between trained warriors. These gladiators were the professional athletes of their day. But although they were celebrities, most gladiators were slaves or prisoners of war forced into fighting for the bloodthirsty crowd's amusement. And they often fought to the death. Rome's emperors hosted these expensive events—which were often free to the public—to make the citizens happy and thus easier to rule.

THE JOUST

Hosted in special arenas called lists within castle walls or in nearby fields, the joust was one of the most thrilling forms of entertainment in the 14th and 15th centuries. Two mounted knights in gleaming armor spurred their warhorses at each other in a ferocious charge. Just before the moment of impact, they leveled their 12-foot (4-m) lances and—crash!—the weapons splintered against shield and helm (a knight scored points in a joust by shattering his lance against his opponent's shield or helm—or knocking him off his horse).

The joust was part of a larger event called the tournament, which evolved from military training into a spectator sport for lords, ladies, and peasants alike. Despite strict rules, tournaments were dangerous games; many knights were maimed or killed in jousts. France's King Henry II died in a joust when a lance pierced his visor. But success in the tournament outweighed the risks for knights, who played for keeps. A victor won the loser's armor and horse, which could be ransomed for a small fortune. The tournament champion might win the favor of a lady in the stands.

ULAMA

As far back as 1400 B.C., people in Mexico and Central America suited up in painted deerskins and elaborate headdresses and sprinted across stone courts to volley a rubber ball with their hips, knees, shins, elbows, and heads. Sounds like a full-court version of Hacky Sack, right? But the ball in this game—known as *ulama* in modern versions—was more like a weapon. Weighing as much as nine pounds (4 kg) and made of solid rubber, the ball left players bruised and bloody. Games resulted in broken bones and even death as players dove to the stone court to keep the ball from touching the ground. Many of the ball courts remain today, some with stone rings that may have acted as goals.

The athletes played for religious reasons: The games were thought to represent the battle of good against evil. Some matches may have ended in sacrificial rituals to appease the gods— and it wasn't always the losers who were sacrificed. It was considered a great honor to die for the gods, so players may have competed for the right to die.

PARTING SHOTS

The Deadly Deal of the DUEL

It started with an insult and ended when one man shot (or stabbed) another at close range. Yet the attacker never went to jail. Instead, he was hailed a winner. And so went the duel, a deadly deal struck between two men (duelists were nearly always men) to resolve a dispute by calmly standing face to face, drawing pistols (or swords), and attacking each other. Today, people might hire lawyers to settle disagreements in court or simply argue in online message boards and let public opinion decide the victor, but from the Middle Ages up to the early 20th century, men from the upper crust of European and American society relied on one-on-one combat to seek resolution for even minor slights to their reputations.

Although not all duels were to the death, thousands of men—including famous politicians and military commanders—perished from injuries received in these ghastly grudge matches. Abraham Lincoln escaped a sword duel by apologizing to a local politician he had offended in a newspaper story. Even after duels were outlawed, deaths were still common and victors were often pardoned—as long as they followed the rules. Duelists adhered to a strict code of conduct (known as the code duello, a document typically kept inside every gentleman's pistol case). To break the rules meant bringing shame on your name, which many considered a fate worse than death.

Until the 17th century, most duels were fought with special swords called rapiers and foils (most nobles were expert swordsmen). Later duels were settled with flintlock pistols, which tended to shoot in wild directions—if they shot at all (the pistols often misfired). As a result, people rarely died in pistol duels. These gun battles were different from the quick-draw duels of the American West.

DUMB REASONS FOR REAL DUELS ...

- An argument over the correct spelling of a Greek word
- Dancing the waltz the wrong way
- A wet dog shaking itself dry on the dresses of two friends
- One man calling another "puppy" (an act that spawned two duels)

TIM
THE GRIM REAPER'S
FATAL FACTS

Before he became the seventh president of the United States, Andrew Jackson engaged in as many as 100 duels. In one controversial 1806 grudge match, he was shot inches from his heart but managed to survive.

A DUEL'S RULES

THE INITIAL INSULT
Any comment that questioned a gentleman's character could spawn a duel. Accusing someone of lying, calling him a scoundrel, accusing his wife or girlfriend of behaving badly, striking someone in a fight—all were serious offenses that demanded "satisfaction."

THE GAUNTLET IS THROWN
The offended gentleman, either in person or through a trusted friend known as a second, officially challenged his foe to a duel. He could do so by throwing a glove at his enemy's feet—a custom inspired by medieval knights who challenged foes by tossing armored gloves known as gauntlets to the ground.

THE ARRANGEMENTS ARE MADE
The duelists' seconds tried their best to resolve the dispute without violence (until the start of combat, duels could be called off if the challenged party apologized). In the meantime, the seconds set up the duel. The challenged party typically chose the weapons along with the time and place of combat.

THE DUEL IS DONE
On the day of the duel, the participants met at the chosen location along with their seconds, who monitored the combat for fair play (on rare occasions, the seconds even battled each other side-by-side with the principal parties). In a pistol duel, the combatants often started back-to-back, walked a set number of paces, then turned and fired within three seconds (to take aim any longer was dishonorable). In a sword duel, the men drew their swords and attacked. Duels might be fought until blood was drawn, until one of the participants was too wounded to continue, or to the death.

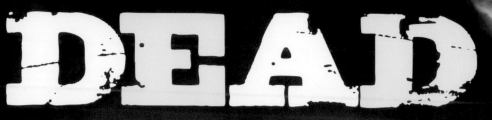

DEAD

Five EXTINCTION EVENTS you'll be happy you missed ...

WHEN IT COMES TO THE SURVIVAL OF LIFE ON EARTH, CHANGE IS BAD. Specifically, catastrophic change: an upheaval that happens over the course of a few thousand or million years—a mere blink of an eye in geological time. More than 90 percent of the animals that have ever lived on Earth have gone extinct, and most of these die-offs happen gradually, with older species fading away as the environment gradually changed and new species evolving to fill the niche they left behind. But once in a great while, the world suffers a calamity—such as an asteroid impact or a sudden change in climate—that wipes out at least 50 percent of life on Earth in a relatively brief amount of time. Five of these extinction events have occurred in the last 500 million years. (Some scientists believe we're experiencing one now.) Lucky for you, life bounced back after each of these events. Otherwise, you wouldn't be reading about these dark days right now ...

440 MILLION YEARS AGO

ORDOVICIAN-SILURIAN EXTINCTION

CREATURES KILLED OFF
85 PERCENT OF MARINE ANIMALS

Life this long ago was still limited largely to the oceans, home to the ancestors of fish, snails, octopuses, squids, crabs, and bugs, along with the first simple vertebrates (animals with a backbone). An ice age triggered the sudden formation of glaciers, which caused sea levels to drop and altered the chemistry of the oceans. Many of the world's sea creatures—including shelled animals, conodonts (similar to eels), and trilobites perished during two massive extinction events hundreds of thousands of years apart.

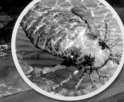

360 MILLION YEARS AGO

LATE DEVONIAN EXTINCTION

CREATURES KILLED OFF
75 PERCENT OF ALL LIFE ON EARTH, ESPECIALLY IN THE SHALLOW SEAS

Like most extinction events, the late Devonian die-off wasn't spawned by a single catastrophe and the ultimate cause remains a mystery. By studying the fossil record, scientists have determined that several major events over the course of 20 million years wiped out 70 percent of all marine animals—especially corals—and dealt a heavy setback to the early creatures on land. Asteroid strikes, changes in the climate and sea levels, and strange soils caused by the first land plant species are among the suspected killers.

250 MILLION YEARS AGO

PERMIAN EXTINCTION

CREATURES KILLED OFF
96 PERCENT OF ALL LIFE ON EARTH

Also known as the Great Dying, this was the largest extinction event in history. Nearly all life on Earth was wiped out over a period of millions of years. Even insects, normally immune to these types of mass die-offs, were hard hit. Scientists aren't sure what caused this deadly period in Earth's history. They suspect the impact of an asteroid or comet, or perhaps cracks in the Earth's crust flooded the land and sea with lava for centuries. Regardless of the cause, we should all feel lucky that any life survived at all. Every plant and animal—including you—that exists today descended from the survivors of the Permian extinction.

ENDS

200 MILLION YEARS AGO

TRIASSIC-JURASSIC EXTINCTION

CREATURES KILLED OFF
50 PERCENT OF ALL SPECIES, PARTICULARLY OCEAN REPTILES, AMPHIBIANS, AND MOST MAMMAL-LIKE ANIMALS

All forms of life from the sea, land, and air were ravaged by this extinction event, caused perhaps by climate change related to lava flows oozing from the earth. Only plants were spared major damage.

65 MILLION YEARS AGO

CRETACEOUS-TERTIARY EXTINCTION

CREATURES KILLED OFF
THE DINOSAURS

Also known as the K/T extinction, the Cretaceous-Tertiary die-off is the most famous and most studied of the five major extinction events. Most scientists agree that a massive asteroid struck the seabed near the Yucatán Peninsula in Mexico, triggering global climate changes that ended the 150-million-year reign of the dinosaurs. This event was also proof that extinction events aren't necessarily bad—at least for the animals that survive. The death of the dinosaurs left a void for smarter, smaller mammals. Suddenly the world was theirs. Mammals grew in size and diversified into many of the species we know today: cats, dogs, horses, bats, rats, and tree-dwelling primates (the order of animals that eventually gave rise to gorillas, chimpanzees, and humans).

RETURN OF THE DEAD:
THE SCIENCE OF DE-EXTINCTION

The woolly mammoth, the dodo bird, the Caribbean monk seal—these animals are gone but not forgotten, hunted to extinction by humans. But science may have a way of undoing our mistakes. Take the woolly mammoth, for instance. Scientists in South Korea and Siberia (where mammoths once roamed in the thousands) have teamed up to "de-extinct" one of these furry, long-tusked elephant relatives, which have been gone for more than 10,000 years. First, the scientists need to extract cells from frozen mammoth carcasses discovered in the tundra. They'll implant these cells in an elephant, which will act as a surrogate mother for a baby mammoth "clone." If all goes well, we could see the return of the woolly mammoth in a matter of years! Or not. We'll see …

ENDS OF THE EARTH

Doomsday

Everything has an expiration date, and that includes life on Earth. In five billion years or so, our sun will run out of fuel—its supply of hydrogen—and swell into an Earth-smothering ball of hot gas. Sometime between now and then, perhaps within the next few thousand years, the world will face more pressing problems. If you're a worrywart, you probably won't want to read about these four ways the world might end before the sun burns out ...

PLIGHT OF THE HONEYBEES

Starting in 2006, beekeepers across the United States noticed an alarming fact about their hives. Honeybees were fleeing their queens and colonies, never to return. The phenomenon—called colony collapse disorder—continued to spread, and by 2013 beekeepers were reporting average losses of 45 percent of their hives. Why should you care if some stinging insects say sayonara? Honeybees are vital pollinators for everything from apples to almonds, avocados to onions (not to mention the source of all honey). They also pollinate the plants that feed livestock animals such as cows, pigs, and chickens. The flight of the honeybees could spell starvation for humans on a global scale. Bee researchers are scrambling to figure out what's causing the disappearing act. Current suspects include parasites, viruses, pesticides, and probably a combination of all three.

PANDEMIC PANIC

Achoo! Uh-oh! The biggest threat to our survival may come from an enemy too small to see with the naked eye: germs. Deadly bacteria and viruses—in the form of widespread infectious outbreaks known as pandemics—have killed more people throughout history than all of the wars combined. Immunizations and advances in medicine protect us from these diseases but can also put us at risk. Scientists fear that overuse of antibiotics—medications that kill dangerous bacteria—is responsible for the rise in "superbugs": germs that resist antibiotics the way Superman can deflect bullets. An especially virulent (or highly contagious) superbug could do big-time damage. Modern air travel means the disease could spread quickly around the globe. Ultimately, the world might end not with a bang, but with a sneeze.

Scenarios

HEAT WAVE

From frigid ice ages to globe-spanning heat waves, Earth's climate has been subject to natural changes throughout its long history. But in the past century or so, temperatures have risen so quickly and consistently that scientists are now certain the causes aren't natural. Why is it happening? Humans burn fossil fuels (coal, oil, and natural gas) to power their homes, cars, planes, and factories. This creates carbon dioxide, which occurs naturally in the atmosphere (animals exhale carbon dioxide, and plants need it for photosynthesis). A so-called greenhouse gas, carbon dioxide traps heat in the atmosphere. Human activity is pumping out so much extra carbon dioxide that we're causing a rapid rise in temperatures across the globe. The decade of 2001–2010 was the warmest ever recorded worldwide.

This increase in heat will lead to more than just some sweaty summers. Melting glaciers and polar ice caps will cause sea levels to rise and low-lying cities and coastal areas to flood. Extreme weather such as hurricanes and tornadoes will become more common. Longer dry seasons and droughts will wipe out crops, leading to starvation. Rising temperatures could result in extinctions that will upset the balance of nature. The side effects of climate change will subside only if humans switch to alternate energy sources (such as solar and wind power), reducing the amount of greenhouse gases we're pumping into the atmosphere.

SPACE INVADERS

Conspiracy theorists are convinced that extraterrestrials (or creatures from other planets) have already stopped by to say hi—and perhaps still walk among us! But even skeptics would have a hard time claiming we're alone in this wide and wild universe. Astronomers have discovered more than 4,000 worlds beyond our solar system and are spotting more every day. Some of these "exoplanets" orbit their stars in the "Goldilocks zone," a distance that's neither too hot nor too cold to support liquid water and possibly alien life. Astronomers at Cornell University predict that as many as 100 million worlds in our galaxy could support complex life.

Whether any of those advanced aliens have developed deep-space travel remains to be seen, but not everyone is ready to welcome E.T. with open arms. Physicist Stephen Hawking, a true believer in alien life, believes we better do everything we can to hide from extraterrestrial astronauts. He fears that alien invaders would ransack Earth for its resources and colonize it. Earthlings would be enslaved or, worse, wiped out. Before calling Hawking a crackpot, keep in mind that he's regarded as the most brilliant scientific mind since Albert Einstein.

TURN THE PAGE FOR THE **SCARIEST DOOMSDAY** SCENARIO OF **ALL!**

TIM THE GRIM REAPER'S FATAL FACTS

The United States' Centers for Disease Control (CDC)—an agency that prepares for pandemics—actually has a plan in place for a "zombie apocalypse" in case the recently deceased rise to eat the living. But before you freak out over the possibility of an undead uprising, relax: The CDC's zombie-preparedness plan is just a publicity stunt.

THE SKY IS FALLING!

WHAT IF ASTEROIDS AND COMETS RAIN DOWN FROM ABOVE ...

It happened before. It will happen again. Someday, a mountain-size rock or slushy ball of ice will fall from the sky and strike the Earth. Seas will boil. Forests will burn. Cities will crumble. Clouds of choking ash will smother the planet. Entire species will go extinct.

Asteroids have smashed into every planet in the solar system. Scientists estimate that more than a million of these itty-bitty worlds orbit the sun in the asteroid belt, a stretch of space between Mars and Jupiter. Some asteroids are large enough to have their own moons. Many are more like rubble piles moving through space—squadrons of small rocks held together by their own gravitational attraction.

These roving rocks are fine when they stay where they belong, orbiting the sun in the loose cluster of the asteroid belt. But when Jupiter's gravity tugs one of the larger asteroids loose and sends it tumbling toward the sun, watch out! Earth's blanket of air protects us from the smaller rocks and chunks of cometary ice. But one good hit from a large space rock or comet could mean game over for life on Earth.

Asteroids travel at tens of thousands of miles an hour—speeds that transfer into destructive energy when they collide with a planet, moon, or each other. A single rock at least 450 feet (137 m) across could destroy an entire city. More than a thousand people were injured in 2013 when an asteroid just 62 feet (19 m) wide exploded high in the atmosphere above Chelyabinsk, Russia. And that was a near

Snowball Fight

Rocks aren't the only rogue bodies roaming the solar system. Comets originate far out in the solar system—some from the Kuiper Belt of icy bodies beyond the orbit of Neptune, and others from a more distant region known as the Oort cloud. Each is an irregular ball of icy slush, frozen gases, and dark minerals just a few miles or kilometers wide. Like asteroids, comets occasionally collide with planets (one slammed into the gas giant Jupiter in 1994) and have the potential to cause massive destruction.

Rock-Stopping Strategies ...

In 2013, NASA announced its Grand Challenge to locate any nasty asteroids heading our way and prevent their impact. Earth-saving options include ...

MELTING IT: Target the asteroid with a space-based laser to vaporize it before it gets too close.

PAINTING IT: Splatter the asteroids with white paint, which would turn the surface into a sail for solar radiation that gradually pushes the asteroid off course.

RAMMING IT: Launch a rocket directly into the asteroid to break it in half or divert it.

TOWING IT: Use the gravitational pull of a large spaceship to "tug" an asteroid off its collision course with Earth.

miss! An asteroid impact 65 million years ago may have wiped out the dinosaurs.

Nobody knows when the next large asteroid will strike, but don't lose any sleep over the thought of a space rock landing in your backyard. Astronomers are using powerful telescopes to scan the skies and track the trajectories of any "near-Earth objects," including asteroids and comets that might drift too close to home. NASA has identified 90 percent of all the near-Earth objects large enough to cause catastrophic damage if they struck our planet. A 1,280-foot (390-m) asteroid—named Apophis after the ancient Egyptian demon of destruction—will swing close to Earth in 2036. Otherwise, we're in the clear. Will our luck hold out forever?

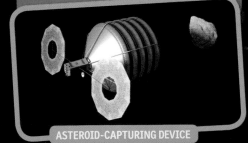

ASTEROID-CAPTURING DEVICE

ALEXANDER HAMILTON VS. AARON BURR

DUEL DATE: JULY 11, 1804   WINNER: AARON BURR

This pistol duel in New Jersey, U.S.A., is the most famous in American history for the political prominence of its participants. Alexander Hamilton was a former U.S. secretary of the treasury. Aaron Burr was the vice president of the United States under Thomas Jefferson. Burr challenged Hamilton to a duel after a particularly nasty election campaign. On the day of the duel, both men drew pistols and fired. Hamilton missed (on purpose, many believe); Burr did not. Shot in the hip, Hamilton died the next day. Dueling had been outlawed in New Jersey, so Burr was charged with murder. His case never went to trial, however, and he served out the rest of his term as vice president.

LADY ALMERIA BRADDOCK VS. MRS. ELPHINSTONE

DUEL DATE: 1792   WINNER: LADY ALMERIA BRADDOCK

Although duelists were nearly always men, women occasionally took up arms to settle disputes. History records one such grudge match between London nobles Lady Almeria Braddock and a certain Mrs. Elphinstone. Claiming that Elphinstone made a comment about her age during a social visit, Braddock challenged her to a pistol duel in Hyde Park. Both women missed, although Elphinstone's shot went through Braddock's hat. The duo then drew swords and continued the fight. Known as the Petticoat Duel, the battle ended when Elphinstone yielded after being stabbed in the arm. She agreed to write an apology.

MONSIEUR DE GRANDPRÉ VS. MONSIEUR LE PIQUE

DUEL DATE: JUNE 22, 1808   WINNER: MONSIEUR DE GRANDPRÉ

When two hot-headed Frenchmen vied for the affection of a young Parisian dancer, it led to the oddest duel in history. The jealous men challenged each other to a gun duel high above the skies of Paris in identical hot-air balloons. Each agreed to aim only at his opponent's balloon rather than his body. On the day of the duel, the men ascended half a mile (0.8 km) above Paris, then fired at each other's balloon using a blunderbuss (a type of shotgun) from a distance of 80 yards (73 m). De Grandpré had the better aim. His shot pierced le Pique's balloon, which collapsed and plummeted to Earth, killing Pique and his unfortunate second who'd come along for the ride.

BLAST-OFF: Unusual DUELS

SUDDEN DEATH

RUN FOR YOUR LIFE!

DANGER ZONE

RISKY BUSINESS

Permian Extinction

Asteroid Strikes

Global Pandemics

Pirates

Gladiator Games

Duels

KILL-O-METER

POISONOUS PAST

TIM
THE GRIM REAPER
RANKS HISTORY'S MOST TERRIFYING TOPICS

CHAPTER 2

Jaws and Claws

A WAR IS RAGING IN THE WILD, pitting sharks against seals, lynxes against hares, snakes against mice, mice against plants, and sometimes even plants against mice! This chapter takes you to the front lines of this creature conflict, in which the combatants evolve new weapons (unlimited teeth!) and defenses (toxic spines!) in a constant arms race to eat and avoid being eaten. The food chain is no place for the faint of heart— especially when humans aren't at the top.

Feeding Frenzy

Sharks rule the sea, but should you fear them?

THE OCEAN IS A DANGEROUS PLACE. ROGUE WAVES BASH BOATS. Rip currents yank sunbathers and surfers out to sea. Sunken-ship survivors die of thirst or exposure to the frigid water as they bob in the boundless ocean awaiting rescue. Compared to these dangers, shark attacks are nothing to worry about. Far more people are injured by their toilets each year than a hungry shark. And for every person who dies in the jaws of Jaws, about two million sharks perish at the hands of humans. You shouldn't fear sharks; sharks should fear you!

But no doubt about it: Sharks are deadly creatures. More than 400 million years of evolution have fine-tuned these fish into perfect predators. Fortunately, you're not on the shark's menu. Researchers believe attacks on people are typically a case of mistaken identity. A shark sees a swimmer's hands or feet flash in the murk and confuses them for the scales of a tasty fish. A surfer is a dead ringer for a sea lion or turtle when spotted from below. Most shark attacks on humans are bite-and-runs—a quick taste of wet suit or surfboard or bony flesh that tells the shark it has munched on the wrong animal. A bump from a small species—blacktips and spinner sharks—might result in a few stitches. Bump-and-runs from the big sharks (opposite page) are much more serious.

Shark attacks on humans have increased in the last 50 years, but that's only because the number of people frolicking in the ocean has skyrocketed. Meanwhile, shark populations are dwindling around the world. These fearsome fish are essential scavengers in the ocean ecosystem. Treat them with respect and you'll get along with them just fine.

THE **TERROR** TRIO

TIGERS: Sometimes called the garbage cans of the ocean, tiger sharks will munch on anything that crosses their snouts—turtles, mollusks, and sometimes people.

BULLS: These stocky sharks are famous for their aggressive attitudes. They can also swim in both fresh and salt water. Imagine jumping in a river and getting bitten by a bull shark. It's happened!

GREAT WHITES: Responsible for more attacks on humans than any other shark, the white's massive size—sometimes more than 20 feet (6 m) long—and powerful jaws (containing as many as 3,000 teeth stacked in its mouth) often result in serious injuries. These sharks are also famous for breaching—leaping out of the water as they ambush prey from below—in some parts of the world.

TIM FATAL FACTS
THE GRIM REAPER'S

The teeth of a great white are so sharp that people can shave with them.

SHARK BITES

SINK YOUR TEETH INTO THESE FINNED FACTS ...

SMELLING RED

A shark's sense of smell is up to 10,000 times more powerful than yours. Some species of sharks can detect a drop of blood in an Olympic-size swimming pool!

INVISIBILITY CLOAKS

A rise in fatal attacks along the Western Australian coastline (a hunting ground for great white sharks) resulted in wet suits designed to make surfers, divers, and snorkelers "invisible" to sharks—or at least appear unappetizing.

NIGHT SIGHT

Although they're color-blind, sharks have excellent vision in low-light conditions. That's one reason sharks may mistakenly bite humans. They can spot swimmers in the murk but can't make out all the details.

SUPER SHARK

You think the great white is a frightening fish? It's small fry compared to the megalodon, a prehistoric predator that prowled the seas as recently as 1.5 million years ago and once preyed on dinosaurs. The megalodon was a supersize version of the great white, reaching nearly 60 feet (18 m) in length. Fossils of its one-foot (30-cm)-long teeth have washed up on beaches across the world.

SIXTH SENSE

The heads of sharks (and rays) are covered with special pores that detect the electrical signals given off by all living things. In other words, sharks can read your heartbeat, muscle movements, and even your brain activity!

SEVENTH SENSE

Sensors alongside a shark's body can read slight pressure changes in the water, such as the flailing of an injured fish—or a human swimmer.

WARNING

DANGEROUS MARINE LIFE ARE COMMON TO THIS AREA

FIN LAND

New Smyrna Beach in Florida, U.S.A., is the shark-attack capital of the world (although some beaches off Hawaii, U.S.A., are gunning for that title). Most people who have swum here have been within 10 feet (3 m) of a shark.

DANGER ZONE

The most likely time and place to have a run-in with a shark is the waters off Florida in September between 2 p.m. and 3 p.m.

A REAL MOUTHFUL

A shark's upper and lower jaws are stacked with rows of razor-sharp teeth. If one tooth falls out, a new one moves from behind to take its place. Sharks lose and replace as many as 2,000 teeth each year!

DEADLiEST
CATCH

LETHAL LIONFISH ARE CONQUERING NEW TERRITORY ...

AN ALIEN INVADER IS ON A MISSION TO EXTERMINATE ALL LIFE IN THE WARM WATERS OF THE SOUTH ATLANTIC AND CARIBBEAN SEA. AND IT'S SUCCEEDING. THE INVADER IS CALLED THE LIONFISH, AND IT CERTAINLY LOOKS THE PART OF A CREATURE FROM ANOTHER WORLD.
Venomous spines sprout from fins and skin covered in red, black, and white stripes. Two beady eyes set above a jutting jaw scan the hollows of reefs and corals for prey. Featherlike fins on the lionfish's sides fan out to funnel fish into gobbling range. When the lionfish pounces, its victims don't stand a chance.

This fearsome fish is a long way from home. Lionfish are native to the Indian and Pacific Oceans, where their numbers are kept in check by predators that have evolved to gobble them up despite their toxic spines. But in the mid-1980s, aquarium owners in Florida, U.S.A., became fed up with their pets' bottomless appetite and dumped them in the nearest body of water: the Atlantic Ocean. Here, the lionfish has neither enemies nor competition for food. It reproduces faster than most native fish, can grow up to 15 inches (38 cm) long, lives up to 20 years,

and doesn't stop hunting until all the smaller fish in the area are wiped out.

Lionfish populations boomed and spread quickly to the Caribbean. In some areas, the numbers of native fish plunged 80 percent. Lionfish are devouring prey that serve as food for larger fish and maintain the health of coral reefs. Some scientists consider these invaders the greatest danger to the tropical seas of the South Atlantic and Caribbean.

But not all hope is lost. Throughout their invasive range, lionfish have attracted a new predator: humans. Armed with spear guns and spine-proof gloves, snorkelers and scuba divers are hunting lionfish throughout the warm waters of the Caribbean and the Atlantic Ocean. Lionfish have become a prize catch in fishing derbies and on restaurant menus. Like any good sci-fi movie, the humans are turning the tide against the alien invaders. The hunter has become the hunted.

TIM
THE GRIM REAPER'S
FATAL FACTS

A lionfish's stomach can expand to 30 times its normal size, letting it gorge on fish around the clock.

STICKER SHOCK

The lionfish doesn't use its prickly parts to attack; they're strictly for protection. Each of the fish's 18 spines injects venom into any creature unlucky enough to brush against it. Although it's not deadly to humans, the toxin still hurts, causing a throbbing pain that lasts a day and can lead to breathing problems.

FOREIGN THREATS
FOUR UNSTOPPABLE INVASIVE SPECIES

The lionfish from the last page are what scientists call an invasive species, meaning they've been introduced to a foreign ecosystem by artificial means. Sometimes they arrive in the ballast of ships, or they're accidentally released by pet owners, or they're dumped overboard by fishermen who use them as bait. Invasive species can spell disaster for their new habitats, where they often have no natural predators and can throw the balance of nature out of whack. Famous invasive species include ...

KUDZU

WHERE IT'S SUPPOSED TO BE: Asia
WHERE IT'S NOT SUPPOSED TO BE: southern United States

WHAT'S THE DAMAGE? Imported to prevent soil erosion in the 1930s, this bright green vine quickly grew out of control during the hot summers and mild winters of the American South. With no natural predators, kudzu vines overwhelmed power lines, buildings, and trees, earning the reputation of "the vine that ate the South."

BURMESE PYTHON

WHERE IT'S SUPPOSED TO BE: South and Southeast Asia
WHERE IT'S NOT SUPPOSED TO BE: the swamps of Florida, U.S.A.

WHAT'S THE DAMAGE? These exotic snakes became popular as pets in the 1990s—until owners discovered that their new pets grew up to 20 feet (6 m). One of the five largest snakes in the world, the Burmese pythons were released into an environment completely unprepared for their voracious appetites. The snakes thrived in the Florida Everglades, where they feed on endangered mammals and even the occasional alligator.

CANE TOAD

WHERE IT'S SUPPOSED TO BE: southern United States, Central America, and northern South America

WHERE IT'S NOT SUPPOSED TO BE: northeastern Australia

WHAT'S THE DAMAGE? It's a classic invasive-species scenario. The government of Australia imported 3,000 cane toads to Queensland in 1935 to control insects that eat sugarcane crops. It turns out the toads ate everything but the pests. A cane toad will devour anything it can pummel with its tongue and cram into its massive mouth. What's worse, cane toads secrete a toxin from glands in their shoulder blades. The toxin can kill any predator—including crocodiles—that chomps the toad.

SNAKEHEAD

WHERE IT'S SUPPOSED TO BE: eastern Asia

WHERE IT'S NOT SUPPOSED TO BE: ponds, lakes, and rivers in California, Florida, and the Atlantic Coast of the United States

WHAT'S THE DAMAGE? Imported to the United States as an aquarium pet and food in fish markets, the nightmarish snakehead became a terror in the rivers and lakes where it was accidentally released. Like a freshwater version of the lionfish, the snakehead reproduces quickly, has a ravenous appetite, and lacks predators. It gobbles up the native fish and has even been known to bite humans. With its sharklike teeth, serpentlike head, ravenous appetite, and ability to walk on land, this monster earned the nickname "Frankenfish."

AWW, Cute!

These **adorable** animals are actually **deadly!**

SLOW LORIS

Aww, Cute!

This tree-climbing creature isn't a character from a Dr. Seuss book, but it sure looks the part! A nocturnal (or active-at-night) primate with oversize eyes and a laid-back lifestyle, the slow loris creeps through the treetops of South and Southeast Asia.

Oh, No!

Resist the urge to snuggle with a slow loris. It's one of the few mammals with a poisonous bite! The loris smears its teeth with toxins secreted from glands near its armpits. Its bites are painful at best and deadly at worst (victims could suffer from a fatal allergic reaction). The loris covers its cute babies with the poison to make predators steer clear.

POLAR BEAR

Aww, Cute!

Covered in fluffy fur from head to paw (and even on the pads of their paws) to keep cozy in their frigid Arctic realm, polar bears—and, especially, their pups—have become icons of cuteness in cartoons, commercials, books, and movies.

Oh, No!

That fluffy fur isn't so fetching when it's smeared red with the blood of prey. Immensely powerful, polar bears are the largest land predators and experts at hunting seals. They show little fear around humans, which leads to tragic results in places where people and polar bears must coexist.

OH, No!

HIPPOPOTAMUS

Aww, Cute!

This mammoth mammal appears gentle—almost sweet—as it lounges in African rivers and munches on vegetation with the rest of its herd. Baby hippos are especially adorable!

Oh, No!

Despite their klutzy appearance, hippos are graceful swimmers and able to match the speed of a human on land. That combined with their territorial nature and bad tempers means danger for anyone who paddles a boat over a submerged hippo herd. Hippos have even been spotted killing Nile crocodiles in one bite. Some people in Africa believe the hippo kills more humans—hundreds per year—than any other large animal.

BOTTLENOSE DOLPHIN

Aww, Cute!

Intelligent, curious, playful, and perpetually smiling (an illusion created by their fixed facial expression), bottlenose dolphins are the most lovable creatures in the sea.

Oh, No!

Dolphins have been documented saving humans from shark attacks and drowning, but these marine mammals have a mean streak, too. They attack and kill porpoises by the hundreds and use their noses to bludgeon smaller animals. People who try to swim with dolphins have been bumped and bitten, as well. As with any wild animal, dolphins are unpredictable and potentially dangerous. You don't need to fear Flipper—just treat him with respect.

SNAP SHOTS
NATURE'S MIGHTIEST
BITES

HORNS AND CLAWS CAUSE ALL KINDS OF HURT, BUT SOMETIMES AN ANIMAL'S MOST LETHAL WEAPONS ARE RIGHT UNDER ITS NOSE (WHICH IS WHY YOU MIGHT RECONSIDER THAT CAREER IN WILDLIFE DENTISTRY). HERE WE'VE ASSEMBLED THE CHAMPIONS OF CHOMP, RANKED IN ASCENDING ORDER OF BITE FORCE MEASURED IN POUNDS PER SQUARE INCH (PSI). PLEASE KEEP YOUR ARMS AND LEGS AWAY FROM THE PAGE AT ALL TIMES ...

**BITE FORCE:
267 PSI**

**BITE FORCE:
169 PSI**

**BITE FORCE:
174 PSI**

GRIZZLY BEAR

Researchers estimate that one grizzly possesses the strength of five humans—even more if the bear gets angry. (They're like the Incredible Hulks of the animal kingdom!) A thousand-pound (454-kg) bear can toss a 700-pound (318-kg) garbage bin like a beach ball! All that might translates to the bear's bite, among the strongest of any mammal.

SPOTTED HYENA

This doglike beast (which is actually more closely related to cats) has a bite much worse than its bark. Famous for devouring every morsel of its scavenged meals, spotted hyenas need strong jaws to crush bones and defend their dinners on Africa's savannas. And don't let their funny guffawing bark fool you; like every other mighty biter ranked here, hyenas have attacked humans.

BIG CATS

It's no surprise that the four "big cat" species—lions, tigers, jaguars, and leopards—also have big bites, so let's lump them together to keep them from overrunning the top five. Lions have the strongest bite, while jaguars are more powerful relative to their size (they need fearsome fangs to bite through the skulls of animals, their preferred method of killing). Leopards have an itty-bitty bite compared to the other three, but they make up for it with their amazing strength and stellar stalking skills. Bengal tigers are the most dangerous, responsible for killing more humans than the other three species.

BIG FANG THEORIES

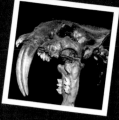

SABER-TOOTHED SURPRISE: Surely the saber-toothed cat—a fearsome predator that prowled North America 10,000 years ago—had a bite to match its famous foot-long (30-cm) incisors, but researchers believe that Smilodon had relatively wimpy choppers. Instead of raw bite force, it relied on its swordlike canines to do its killing.

AMAZONIAN ASSASSIN: The award for history's biggest bite actually goes to a small fish: the Amazon River's black piranha. But there's a catch: This 15-inch (38-cm) predator has the strongest bite relative to its size. A black piranha can bite with a force equal to 30 times its body weight. Not even prehistoric predators the *Tyrannosaurus rex* or the megalodon super shark came close to matching the piranha's "bite force quotient."

MARINE MYSTERY: You'd think a great white shark—with its nearly limitless supply of serrated choppers—would have the most awesome jaws in the animal kingdom. But the verdict is still out. A 2008 computer simulation predicted that a 21-foot (6.4-m) great white shark could top a croc's bite with a force of nearly 4,000 psi, but the results have yet to be replicated in real life. After all, would you volunteer to test the jaws of the villain in *Jaws*?

BITE FORCE: 3,700 PSI

BITE FORCE: 1,821 PSI

HIPPOPOTAMUS

On page 45 you read that the fiercely territorial hippopotamus is one of Africa's most dangerous creatures—and here's one big reason why: Its massively muscled jaw—which at full yawn opens nearly 180 degrees—delivers the second mightiest snap in the animal kingdom.

CROCODILE

A crocodile's smile holds the boldest bite of all, and the saltwater croc takes the record for the world's most damaging dentition. Turn the page to read all about these titans of tooth.

TIM
THE GRIM REAPER'S
FATAL FACTS

Peer in the mirror and smile! It turns out those pearly whites pack an impressive bite. According to one study, our molars have a stronger bite force—relative to our size—than that of our relatives the gorilla, chimpanzee, and other primates. So that's why it stings so much when I bite my tongue.

BEWARE OF CROCS!

THE TOOTHY TRUTH BEHIND THESE FRIGHTFUL REPTILES ...

A DEADLY BEAST LURKS JUST BELOW THE MURKY SURFACE of rivers, swamps, and seas across the tropical regions of the world. It once hunted dinosaurs. Today, it lies in wait for any unfortunate animal—wildebeest, deer, baby hippo, human—that steps too close to the water's edge. And when this beast rears its scaly head ... snap! Few creatures escape its jaws, the strongest of any living animal.

THREE KILLER CROCODILIANS

AMERICAN ALLIGATOR

Common in swamps, rivers, and lakes in the southern portions of the United States, these scaly reptiles have shorter, rounder snouts than their crocodile cousins. Less aggressive than crocodiles, alligators are still dangerous and have attacked humans.

NILE CROCODILE

These massive African crocodilians are famous for feasting on the wildebeests that scamper across the Nile during migration season. Nile crocs can hold their breath underwater for two hours waiting to ambush prey. They're blamed for killing up to 200 people every year.

CROCODILIANS—an order of reptiles that includes crocodiles and alligators—are efficient killing machines, honed through 85 million years of evolution. They are considered "ambush predators" because of the way they slink through the shallows, holding their breath for more than an hour, waiting for prey to wander by. These brutes then use their powerful tails to explode from the water, lock on with vice-like jaws, and drag their victims into the depths until they drown. Crocodile prey never see the attacks coming.

BUDDY AND THE BEAST

NOT ALL CROCS ARE KILLERS. Gilberto "Chito" Shedden made a friend for life when he found a wounded crocodile (it had been shot in the eye) on the shore of a Costa Rican river in 1989 and nursed it back to health. Chito named the croc Pocho, and he soon began swimming with his fearsome fanged friend. Crowds gathered to watch the two frolic in the water. Pocho eventually grew to 16 feet (5 m) before finally dying of old age in 2011. People from across Costa Rica attended Pocho's funeral.

CROCS ROCKED

This hungry river otter in Florida figured out how to kill a 5-foot (1.5-m) alligator by gnawing on the back of its neck.

A 10-foot (3.5-m) olive python in Australia gulped down a 3-foot (1-m) crocodile after squeezing it to death. This snake fared better than a 13-foot (4-m) python that burst after trying to eat a 6-foot (2-m) alligator in the Florida Everglades in 2006.

SALTWATER CROCODILE

The largest of the crocodilians, "salties" prowl the waters of eastern India, Southeast Asia, and northern Australia. They've been spotted far out to sea and have been known to attack people—and even sharks.

WHAT A CROC! A "salty" named Lolong was the largest saltwater crocodile ever captured alive. More than 20 feet (6 m) long and 2,370 pounds (1,075 kg) of muscle, teeth, and heavily armored hide, he was suspected of killing two people in the Philippines.

GREEN GOBBLERS

Meet the MEAT-EATING plants ...

Look at the bright side the next time your parents tell you to eat your vegetables—at least your vegetables aren't eating you! Hundreds of species of plants are carnivorous, meaning they eat meat. But don't worry about becoming dinner for a dandelion; carnivorous plants are deadly only to morsel-size animals: flies, mice, lizards, frogs, and the occasional unlucky bird.

Plants don't have brains, bellies, or muscles. So why did carnivorous plants develop a taste for animals, and how do they capture their snacks? Like all other plants, these chompers soak energy from the sun and slurp nutrients from the soil. But because they tend to grow in nutrient-poor dirt (such as rocky spots or acidic swamps), meat-eating plants developed the ability to supplement their diets. Bugs and the itty-bitty bodies of other animals give these plants the nutritional boost they need to grow leaves for capturing energy from the sun. Evolution has armed them with a wild and wide variety of traps for capturing, killing, and devouring dinner, turning sorry soils into gardens of eatin'. See for yourself ...

PITCHER PLANTS
With leaf structures disguised as pitchers of sweet nectar, these plants lure hungry insects and other small animals that stop by for a drink. Victims tumble into the pitcher, where they're trapped by tiny hairs and digested into goo by special chemicals.

STICKY PLANTS
Like the tentacles of an octopus, the sticky leaves of butterworts, sundews, and similar plants snare insects, which are slowly digested as they decompose.

SUCTION PLANTS

Think of these plants as vacuums made of vegetation. The aquatic bladderwort is the best example. By pumping the water out of its tiny bladders, it can suck in passing water fleas and mosquito larvae faster than you can blink.

TRAPPING PLANTS

The Venus flytrap is the most famous of this type, which has leaves lined with interlocking hairs that snap shut when disturbed by insects. Once sprung, a trapping plant becomes a sort of short-term stomach where the bug is boiled down into nutrients.

TIM
THE GRIM REAPER'S
FATAL FACTS

Some pitcher plants are larger than real drink pitchers—large enough to hold two gallons (7.6 L) of sweet nectar. Their massive size is deep trouble for any lizards, frogs, mice, or birds that tumble in but can't escape.

SEEING RED!

The African buffalo is one bad bull ...

THE LIONS WERE ROOKIES, OR RECKLESS, OR JUST REALLY HUNGRY, BUT THEY PICKED ON THE WRONG PREY WHEN THEY POUNCED ON A BABY AFRICAN BUFFALO IN SOUTH AFRICA'S KRUGER NATIONAL PARK. In a blur of golden fur—and in a famous sequence captured on video in 2004—the lions chased the calf away from its herd. Splash! The lead lion knocked the calf into a watering hole before five other lions in pursuit piled on top of it. A pair of crocodiles joined the fray, locking jaws on the panicked calf and using its body to play tug-of-war with the lions.

Then the baby buffalo's daddy showed up, and he brought friends.

Africa's lions and crocodiles know better than to tussle with an African buffalo. Although these big, bold beasts (which weigh half as much as the family car) graze on grass like other kinds of cattle and don't have sharp teeth or tusks, they're among Africa's deadliest animals. African buffalo are one of the so-called Big Five (along with lions, elephants, rhinos, and leopards) that have been known to track down and attack big-game hunters who accidentally wound the animal instead of killing it.

A lion, leopard, or other top predator would never dare to challenge an adult African buffalo. Buffalo are just too tenacious! Calves, on the other hand, are an easier target if the big cats can separate the baby buffalo from the herd. There's just one problem: A calf in distress will call for help. When it does, the herd comes running. That's exactly what happened at the so-called Battle of Kruger. The calf's cries attracted a male—or bull—buffalo. It attacked the lead lion with its horns, making the big cat catch big air. The calf escaped into the safety of the herd while the rest of the lions scampered. They learned an important lesson: Never get on the bad side of an African buffalo.

BULKY BODY

Buffalo are strong enough to launch full-grown lions into the air and tip over safari trucks.

HORN HELMET

The horns of bull buffalo connect above the head in a plate that can block bullets.

MENACING MEMORY

African buffalo remember hunters and animals that have wronged them in the past. In other words, they bear a grudge.

SPEED DEMONS

Although bulky, buffalo can run up to 35 miles an hour (56 km/h)—much faster than a panicked hunter.

THICK SKIN

The hide of a buffalo's neck is thick enough to deflect the horns of other bulls (although it's not tough enough to stop rhinoceros horns).

IF LOOKS COULD KILL

THESE HARMLESS CREATURES ONLY LOOK DEADLY ...

LEATHERBACK SEA TURTLE

Ask the world's largest turtle to open wide and say *"ahhh"* and you'll see a mouth straight out of a monster movie, crammed with spiky teeth that line the walls of its throat. The spikes help the gentle leatherback snap up and trap fish.

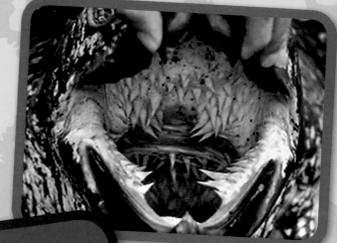

BASKING SHARK

You'd think any shark with a mouth massive enough to fit a motorcycle would send everyone at the beach scurrying for shore. Relax! The basking shark—the second largest fish in the world—eats nothing bigger than itty-bitty plankton, which it strains from the water with its 3-foot (1-m)-wide mouth.

GHARIAL

Unlike its man-eating alligator and crocodile cousins, this Indian crocodilian is no threat to humans. Its skinny snout is too fragile to bite anything bigger than fish.

AYE-AYE

This gentle native of the island of Madagascar is only dangerous to insects, which it digs from tree branches with its extralong middle finger. Unfortunately, superstitious humans sometimes kill this harmless primate out of fear of its sinister appearance.

MILK SNAKE

Adopting a type of camouflage known as defensive mimicry, the harmless milk snake is a cunningly colored clone of the coral snake: North America's most venomous snake. A milk snake's skin has red stripes next to black ones; if you spot a snake with yellow stripes alongside red ones, keep your distance—it's a killer coral snake!

HARD TO KILL

TARDIGRADES

These itty-bitty eight-legged beasts (no bigger than the period at the end of this sentence) can shrug off subzero temperatures, sunbathe in deadly radiation, and go a decade without a drink. In fact, scientists study tardigrades for their toughness. They ride out droughts and deep freezes by shutting down their bodies and rolling into balls that look like microscopic boogers. While in this switched-off state, tardigrades are virtually indestructible. They revive in water and resume their lumbering business as if nothing bad ever happened—even after a decade of deactivation.

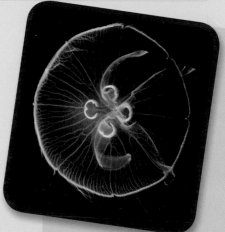

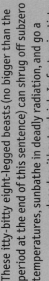

COCKROACHES

They've crept through Earth's crannies for 300 million years and survived the worldwide calamity that wiped out the dinosaurs. Cockroaches keep on crawling and crawling and crawling for all sorts of creepy reasons. They're more active at night, when it's easier to hide from predators. The roughly 4,500 species of roaches around the world have evolved to fill nearly every ecological niche (including humid sewers, where they reproduce by the millions). Hardier than most insects, roaches are resistant to radiation and can go a month between meals. And they'll eat almost anything—including human eyelashes!

IMMORTAL JELLYFISH

Although it's not really a jellyfish (technically, it's a hydrozoan), the bell-shaped ball of jelly known as *Turritopsis nutricula* really is capable of living forever. When the going gets tough, it reverts to its earliest stage of development and begins the aging process over again from scratch, essentially hitting the reset button on its life. That would be like you transforming into a baby whenever you wanted.

THREE Extreme SURVIVORS

SUDDEN DEATH	Nile Crocodile
RUN FOR YOUR LIFE!	Hippopotamus
DANGER ZONE	Great White Shark
	African Buffalo
RISKY BUSINESS	Polar Bear
	Lionfish

KILL-O-METER

BLOODTHIRSTY BEASTS

TIM
THE GRIM REAPER
RANKS DEADLY CREATURES

CHAPTER 3

Defying Death

LOOK, UP IN THE SKY! IT'S A IT'S A PLANE! IT'S A ... WAIT,

It's a guy jumping out of a plane! Why would anyone take a flying leap out of a perfectly good aircraft?! Hold on to your lunch—and your limbs—as we soar into the thrilling, terrifying, life-threatening world of daredevils and extreme athletes. From skydiving to cave diving, volcano surfing to the deadliest ways to make a living, we're about to go higher, bigger, and faster into the danger zone, where risk is its own reward.

Extreme surfers
risk it all **for the**
ride of their lives ...

WAVE
GOODBYE

Big-wave hunters hunch over their surfboards in shark-infested waters, staring out to sea for telltale grooves that indicate an incoming swell. When the right wave arrives, looming like a mountain, they paddle, paddle, paddle to build speed before plunging over the wave's frothing lip, popping to their feet, and racing down a sheer face up to 50 feet (15 m) tall. For big-wave surfers, speed is the key. Drop too slowly and they'll get sucked back up the face and swallowed by the crashing wave, spun through the water like a sock in a washing machine. Too much speed and they risk shooting ahead of the wave—directly into the impact zone, where tons of seawater will crash on their heads. Either mistake could be a big-wave surfer's last.

Invented in the Hawaiian Islands, surfing was already an ancient sport when British explorer Captain James Cook first witnessed it in 1778. Although island kings rode savage swells to prove their bravery, the practice of big-wave surfing—paddling into waves at least 20 feet (6 m) tall—didn't grab worldwide attention until the surf movies of the 1950s and '60s. Today, it's a professional sport with sponsors, contests, and cash prizes. Pro surfers must be ready to fly within 24 hours' notice to any of the world's monster-waves spots. Hitting monster-wave status requires the right mix of winds, tides, currents, and storms, which combined can produce waves reaching over 100 feet (30 m) tall.

But while the rewards are high, so is the danger. Wipeouts can lead to hold-downs: punishing, panic-inducing dips to depths of 50 feet (15 m) propelled by the tremendous force of a crashing monster wave. Held-down surfers must navigate underwater reefs and rocks to reach the surface, where a thick layer of choking foam usually awaits. They must catch their breath and clear the impact zone quickly or risk getting slammed by another crashing wave. Double hold-downs are dangerous. Triple hold-downs can kill.

Big-wave surfers—a small, elite group—train to survive these dangers, but monster waves are unpredictable, and so are the creatures that lurk below them. Maverick's—a foggy California, U.S.A., surf break considered the Mount Everest of big-wave surfing—lies in the middle of the Red Triangle, a breeding ground for great white sharks. (At least one Maverick's rider has been attacked.) Even the terminology for this sport is menacing. Surfers ride skinny boards called guns and compete in spots named Jaws and Dungeons and Alligator Rock. You might think these surfers have a death wish, but the opposite is true. Like athletes in other dangerous extreme sports, they feel alive when they're risking death.

PRO SURFER GARRETT MCNAMARA LOOKS LIKE A FLEA ON THE FACE OF THIS 100-FOOT (30-M)-TALL MONSTER—the largest wave ever ridden—off the coast of Nazaré in Portugal. Waves larger than 50 feet (15 m) are too powerful to paddle into, so big-wave surfers clutch the towrope of a zippy watercraft for a speed boost.

TIM
THE GRIM REAPER'S
FATAL FACTS

Some big-wave surfers carry a spare air canister and wear a special vest that works like a sort of underwater parachute. Pulling the rip cord inflates the vest with air and pops the surfer to the surface during deadly hold-downs.

SKILLS, THRILLS, AND SPILLS!

WE CHART A COURSE THROUGH THE MOST DANGEROUS SPORTS FOR EVERY TERRAIN ... (SO YOU DON'T HAVE TO!)

DANGER LEVEL ▶

LAND

FREE SOLOING

Extreme cliff climbers, free soloists reach new heights without relying on safety ropes and harnesses.

NECESSARY SKILLS: The physical strength required to climb vertical surfaces by wedging fingers into cracks, along with the ability to look down from great heights without throwing up.

SAMPLE THRILLS: Dangling from an overhanging cliff face and soaking in spectacular views from the summit.

TYPICAL SPILLS:
Muscle fatigue could lead to falling. (Free soloists can't kick back in their safety harnesses to rest exhausted muscles.)

SEA

CAVE DIVING

The deadliest of the diving sports, cave diving involves squeezing through claustrophobic aquatic caverns in complete darkness.

NECESSARY SKILLS: Training in cave navigation. Nerves of steel when things go wrong with tons of rock between you and the surface.

SAMPLE THRILLS: Exploring stunning labyrinthine cave networks where few have gone before.

TYPICAL SPILLS: Even minor malfunctions or mistakes—such as stirring up sediment and ruining visibility—can end badly.

AiR

WINGSUIT BASE JUMPING

BASE stands for Buildings, Antennas, Spans, and Earth—the types of fixed features from which these daredevils plummet. But these expert skydivers kick up the difficulty and danger of BASE jumping by donning special suits with inflatable flaps that grant limited flight capabilities.

NECESSARY SKILLS: The ability to pilot the wingsuit and pull the rip cord with zero margin for error.

SAMPLE THRILLS: Soaring like Superman while skimming a mountainside and dodging terrain.

TYPICAL SPILLS:
Equipment failures or smacking into a boulder at top speed.

EXTREME

SKATEBOARDING

Pro skaters link tricks in skateparks and drop into U-shaped half-pipe ramps to launch high into the air.

NECESSARY SKILLS: Mastery of basic airborne and "flatland" tricks (such as the ollie, which pops the rider into the air).

SAMPLE THRILLS: Defying gravity off the half-pipe to perform aerial spins (the record, set by high-flying Tony Hawk, stands at two and a half spins, or 900 degrees).

TYPICAL SPILLS: Skinned knees and broken bones from rough landings.

WRECK DIVING

Using specialty scuba gear, these technical divers explore the hulks of sunken ships at dim ocean depths exceeding 610 feet (183 m).

NECESSARY SKILLS: Knowledge of wreck-diving gear, specialized breathing gases, and how to cope with the dangers of deep diving.

SAMPLE THRILLS: Discovering new wrecks and exploring their interiors.

TYPICAL SPILLS: Getting lost inside a wreck or coming down with nitrogen narcosis, a state of confusion caused by breathing at extreme depths.

BASE JUMPING

Standard BASE jumping is a bit safer, but not by much! After all, you're still plummeting to the earth, even if there is a parachute to slow your fall.

NECESSARY SKILLS: Climbing skills (to reach mountaintop launch points) and expert control over free fall flight and parachute gliding.

SAMPLE THRILLS: Plummeting down the sheer side of a cliff or building.

TYPICAL SPILLS: Colliding with rocks or getting parachute cords hung up on obstacles.

PARKOUR

Always in motion, practitioners of this French sport rely on acrobatic moves and sprinting speed to zip from A to B as gracefully as possible.

NECESSARY SKILLS: Gymnastics training, endurance, and the ability to bounce back from a fall.

SAMPLE THRILLS: Running along walls and leaping over obstacles like Spider-Man.

TYPICAL SPILLS: Tumbling off a rooftop or tripping over a guardrail.

FREE DIVING

It's sink and swim in this scary sport that has athletes competing to see who can dive the deepest on one breath.

NECESSARY SKILLS: Amphibious ability to sink to 700 feet (213 m) using fins or weights. Ability to hold breath more than five minutes.

SAMPLE THRILLS: Encountering whales, sharks, and other sea creatures that shy away from scuba divers and their noisy exhaust bubbles.

TYPICAL SPILLS: Passing out from lack of air.

SKYDIVING

Looking while they leap, skydivers plummet from airplanes and deploy parachutes to avoid going splat.

NECESSARY SKILLS: Training in parachute packing, pulling the rip cord before it's too late, and gliding safely to the landing zone.

SAMPLE THRILLS: Experiencing free fall and falling in formation with other skydivers.

TYPICAL SPILLS: Hitting the ground hard after failures of the main or reserve parachute. (Skydivers carry a backup!)

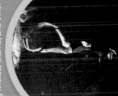

UP AND AWAY!

MEET AN EXTREME ATHLETE WHO CLIMBS MOUNTAINS AND THEN LEAPS FROM THE TOP ...

LIFE FOR STEPHANIE "STEPH" DAVIS IS A SERIES OF UPS AND DOWNS. WHILE MOST EXTREME ATHLETES PRACTICE ONE DANGEROUS SPORT, SHE HAS MASTERED A TRIPLE THREAT: FREE CLIMBING, BASE JUMPING, AND WINGSUIT SKYDIVING. OH, AND SHE'S AN AUTHOR, TOO. IS THERE ANYTHING THAT SCARES THE FIRST WOMAN TO SUMMIT ALL THE SNOWCAPPED PEAKS OF THE FITZ ROY RANGE IN PATAGONIA? TIM THE GRIM REAPER FINDS OUT …

TIM: Something tells me you're not afraid of heights.
DAVIS: Not really.

TIM: You took piano lessons as a kid and learned to play before you got into climbing. Which was more difficult to learn?
DAVIS: They are both hard, in different ways, but they also have a lot of similarities—mainly that you need to practice a lot and enjoy practicing.

TIM: As a free climber, you're not supposed to rely on ropes to help you climb. What do you do if you get tired?
DAVIS: You find a small ledge or a place where you can stand more on your legs than on your arms and try to rest your arms.

TIM: How on Earth do you fall asleep in a portaledge?
DAVIS: Portaledges are really comfortable and always in a beautiful place. You actually sleep really well in them.

TIM: When you started skydiving, was it hard to get used to the idea of falling—something you avoid while climbing?
DAVIS: It was really hard. I think skydiving and BASE jumping can be harder for climbers, because we don't want to fall. But now I like the feeling a lot.

TIM: How did you work up the courage for your first BASE jump?
DAVIS: A lot of preparation is what allows you to feel ready: hundreds of skydives; a lot of practice flying the parachute; doing some jumps from a helicopter, which isn't moving forward like a plane. It was still really scary doing the first BASE jump.

TIM: Why are you drawn to these scary activities?
DAVIS: I enjoy doing things that are outdoors and require a lot of focus. I also like doing things that take a lot of technical ability and take me to high places.

TIM: So what's next for you? Free diving? Swimming with sharks?
DAVIS: I don't like the water; I like the air. It's hard to be good at a lot of things, so climbing, BASE jumping, and wingsuit flying are keeping me pretty busy.

PORTALEDGE

LACK OF AIR

Although expert free divers can hold their breath for up to 22 minutes (the current world record), the average person can only manage 40 seconds before they start sputtering for air. And thanks to something called mammalian diving reflex, an ability shared by all mammals, you can hold your breath longer when you're underwater.

HEAT EXHAUSTION

The average person will overheat—a condition called hyperthermia—after just ten minutes spent in a humid environment exceeding 140 degrees Fahrenheit (60°C). Death soon follows if he or she can't cool off.

SLEEP DEPRIVATION

Avoid going to bed and you'll soon suffer the consequences: crankiness, clumsiness— even hallucinations if you miss a few days of sleep. No one has ever actually died from lack of snoozing, although one man perished after staying awake for 11 days (doctors suspect other factors played a role in his death).

THIRST

A healthy person could survive only five or six days without water— fewer days in hot climates.

STARVATION

People have survived more than ten weeks without food, but they had water and didn't need to move around too much. Starvation takes a horrible toll on the body, however, causing all sorts of unpleasant symptoms, from extreme weakness to hallucinations to spasms.

LIMITS ON LIFE

UNLESS YOU TURN INTO A HULKING GREEN MONSTER WHEN YOU GET GRUMPY OR HAVE INVENTED A SUIT OF SUPERPOWERED ARMOR LIKE TONY STARK, YOU'RE NOT INVINCIBLE. SORRY, BUT THE TRUTH HURTS! SEE FOR YOURSELF IN THIS HEAD-TO-TOE BREAKDOWN OF YOUR BODY'S VULNERABILITIES ...

DEEP TROUBLE

Scuba divers who dive below 130 feet (40 m) risk a lethal buildup of nitrogen bubbles in their bloodstream unless they breathe a special air mixture and make lengthy decompression stops on their return to the surface (but then they risk running out of air).

DEEP FREEZE

Most humans die if their body temperature drops to 70 degrees Fahrenheit (21°C), which can happen if they spend too much time in even slightly chilly water or spend too long out in the cold.

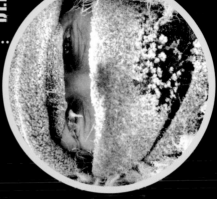

ALTITUDE ILLNESS

Even experienced mountain climbers will die if they spend much time above 26,000 feet (7,925 m) without an oxygen supply.

Courage
ON THE WAY TO CLASS

You won't believe how these kids get to school!

The next time you daydream about Saturday afternoon during your Monday-morning commute to school, look at the bright side: At least you're not clinging to a cliff or crossing a gorge on a rickety cable. In some remote parts of the world, getting to class is a death-defying adventure. The big photo on this page shows one such scary commute. It might look like a thrilling zip-line ride at your local amusement park, but look closer and you'll notice a lack of helmets and harnesses. Such safety features are luxuries for the children of families living in the hills outside Bogotá, Colombia. Their school lies on the opposite side of a canyon, which is linked by steel cables more than 1,300 feet (400 m) high.

Using a loop of rope tied around a pulley as a seat, students zip down the cable at 50 miles an hour (80 km/h), crossing the half-mile (800-m) gorge in about a minute. A crooked tree branch serves as a brake; it smokes and squeaks as riders squeeze it against the cable to bleed speed. (The only time the children don't slide to school is when it rains, which makes the cable too slippery to use.) An old tire at the bottom of the cable provides a rough landing spot. Kids too young to slide on their own climb into a sack carried by their older siblings. They'll learn how to ride the cable soon enough.

Meanwhile, in ...

... CHINA

Pupils hike up, up, and up some more to their primary school halfway to the top of a mountain in China's Guizhou Province. Their headmaster leads them along a ledge no wider than a sidewalk.

... SRI LANKA

Schoolgirls steel their nerves to cross a plank between the walls of Galle Fort, a 16th-century fortress, on their way to school.

... SUMATRA

Daredevil students from the village of Batu Busuk navigate the tightrope that was once a suspension bridge (until it was damaged by a storm) 30 feet (9.1 m) above a rushing river. They then hike another seven miles (11 km) through the dense forest to get to class on time.

TIM
THE GRIM REAPER'S
FATAL FACTS

Elsewhere in China, in the northwestern part of the country, students take a 125-mile (201-km) trek across skinny mountain ledges and four freezing rivers. It takes them two days to reach their school, where they live for the semester.

RISKY BUSINESS
America's Most Dangerous Jobs

DEATHS PER 100,000 FULL-TIME WORKERS PER YEAR

100

80

60

40

20

0

ROOFER >>>>

JOB DESCRIPTION: Fear of heights is not an option for these workers. Roofers clamber up ladders and hug the side of steep roofs to hammer in shingles and pour hot tar in all types of weather, from slick rain to scorching summer afternoons.

ON-THE-JOB HAZARDS: Of all the dangerous construction jobs—including high-rise laborers and electricians—roofers have it the roughest. Accidental falls are one danger, of course, but roofers also succumb to heatstroke while working on dark roof surfaces that turn into frying pans under the summer sun.

39

30

<<<<

GARBAGE COLLECTOR

JOB DESCRIPTION: Driving large trucks on different routes every workday (and typically into the night), these men and women gather and crush all the garbage, compost, tin cans, and plastic bottles you pack into bins on the curb, along with all the waste tossed into the heavy Dumpsters of businesses.

ON-THE-JOB HAZARDS: According to statistics, garbage collectors have a more dangerous job than firefighters or policemen. They work alongside hazardous materials and operate dangerous trash-mashing equipment. But the biggest risk is collision from vehicles whizzing by as they work in the street.

LOGGERS >>>>>

JOB DESCRIPTION: *Timmmberrr!* Lumberjacks lug heavy chain saws deep into the forest to topple tall trees, but that's only half the job. They also use cranes and large trucks to transport all that timber to mills, where it's turned into everything from building lumber to toilet paper.

92

ON-THE-JOB HAZARDS: Just about every aspect of this career—from the tools to the tumbling trees to the rugged landscape—can kill. Lumberjacks also work in the great outdoors, where the nearest emergency room is at least a helicopter ride away.

75

51

PILOTS AND FLIGHT CREWS

JOB DESCRIPTION: Before you get worked up about your next airline flight, keep in mind this broad job category includes pilots and crew who work for private clients and cargo companies, hauling freight and passengers across the country and world.

ON-THE-JOB HAZARDS: Pilots and crew of commercial airliners face few risks during routine flights, while private pilots fly all sorts of airplanes—large and small, new and old—to remote airports with dangerous runways through all types of weather and turbulence, risking mechanical failures and crashes during tricky takeoffs and landings.

COMMERCIAL-FISHING WORKER

JOB DESCRIPTION: Unless you caught it yourself, that tuna on your sandwich or fish stick on your dinner plate once passed through the cargo hold of a commercial fishing boat. These sea-worn workers work with heavy nets, long lines, and giant crab traps on pitching decks in dangerous weather far out to sea.

ON-THE-JOB HAZARDS: The dangers of commercial fishing have been well documented on TV. Shipwrecking storms, accidental drowning, and heavy equipment all contribute to what was once the deadliest job.

(Almost)
LOST in SPACE

HOW APOLLO 13'S ASTRONAUTS SNATCHED TRIUMPH FROM TRAGEDY ...

Despite fail-safe systems and emergency procedures designed to keep them alive, astronauts have one of the world's deadliest jobs. Fourteen American men and women perished in two separate shuttle explosions, and that figure doesn't include astronauts who died during training accidents since the dawn of the space program in the 1950s. The three-man crew of Apollo 13 nearly became the first astronauts to blast off but never return. Launched in 1970, they made up the third mission bound for a moon landing. But despite the danger and spectacle of a space launch, NASA's lunar missions were becoming routine. People on Earth paid little attention to Apollo 13's flight—until disaster struck.

Two days into the mission's four-day voyage to the moon, the crew heard a big bang. Warning lights lit up, electrical systems shut down, and control thrusters sent the spacecraft—composed of two linked parts: the lunar module and the command module—shimmying through space. "Houston, we've had a problem," reported the mission's commander, Jim Lovell. Apollo 13's crew thought they'd been struck by a meteor. Instead, an electrical short had caused an oxygen tank to explode. Mission Control

immediately called off the lunar landing, but that was the least of the crew's problems. They didn't have enough power, water, and air to make it home.

Rescue in space was impossible, so NASA's brightest minds set to work planning how to bring Apollo 13 safely home. The crew used the lunar module as a lifeboat. The stubby craft—about as big inside as a large bedroom closet—was designed to keep two men alive on the moon's surface for two days. Suddenly, it was tasked with supporting three men for four days. The astronauts shut down all unnecessary systems—including heat—to conserve power. Huddling together for warmth, they fired the lunar module's engines to shave hours off their return trip—hours they couldn't afford to waste in space. NASA engineers helped the astronauts improvise filters to remove a deadly buildup of carbon dioxide in the air. Finally, nearly four days after the explosion, the Apollo 13 crew splashed down safely in the South Pacific Ocean. Daring decisions, quick thinking, and ingenuity saved the ship and its crew in what Lovell labeled a "successful failure."

TIM
THE GRIM REAPER'S
FATAL FACTS

Modern technology has made working in space safer, but astronauts will face new dangers—such as micrometeorite impacts and overexposure to radiation— when they travel to Mars and farther in the solar system.

Two Tales of
EXTREME SURVIVAL

DESPERATE MEASURES

More than five days after a boulder pinned his right hand to the wall of a remote slot canyon in Utah, U.S.A., outdoorsman Aron Lee Ralston had run out of food, water, and options. He had even recorded farewells to his family on a video camera. But on the dawn of the sixth day, Ralston resolved that he would survive the experience and see his loved ones again. Using the blade of a multi-tool, he cut off his trapped hand and hiked out of the canyon to find rescue.

HOPE AFLOAT

American sailor Steve Callahan drifted in a life raft for 76 days in the Atlantic Ocean after his sailboat sank (possibly because of a whale attack). Facing certain death from thirst and starvation, Callahan figured out how to catch fish using a broken speargun and improvised lures while keeping his leaky raft afloat using tarps and a sleeping bag. By the time he reached rescue off the coast of Guadalupe Island, Callahan had drifted 1,800 miles (2,897 km) and lost a third of his body weight to hunger and thirst.

NEW SPORTS
WITH OLD
DANGERS

VOLCANO SURFING

Strapping snowboards to their feet or squatting on wooden sleds, volcano surfers race down the slopes of Cerro Negro, an active volcano in Nicaragua. They reach speeds of 30 miles an hour (48 km/h), which makes for skinned knees and bloody elbows if they bail on the gravel-size grains of volcanic rock. Even scarier: Volcano surfers have very little steering control!

SCUBA SKYDIVING

Here's a sport that makes a big splash! Wearing a snorkel (and, of course, a parachute), scuba skydivers jump from a plane high above a coral reef or sunken wreck. Scuba tanks are too heavy to wear parachuting, so the scuba skydiver must stash his breathing gear in the water below. After he or she pulls the rip cord and has a successful splashdown, the diver slips on the diving gear and commences exploring the underwater realm. Oh, and having a boat nearby is essential unless the diver wants to swim home.

HELI-SKIING

When extreme skiers and snowboarders get tired of taking the chairlift to the same lame runs, they hire a helicopter pilot and head out of bounds—way, way out of bounds. A sport for the rich (or professionally sponsored), heli-skiing gives downhill athletes the opportunity to blaze their own trails on a mountain untouched by resort crowds or snow-grooming machines. Aside from the standard dangers inherent in skiing and flying through misty mountains, heli-skiers risk having to outrun any avalanches they might set off in all that fresh pow pow.

KILL-O-METER

LAST **PASTIMES**

TIM
THE GRIM REAPER
RANKS **DEATH-DEFYING ACTIVITIES**

Double **DARES**

SUDDEN DEATH

RUN FOR YOUR LIFE!

DANGER ZONE

RISKY BUSINESS

BASE Wingsuit Jumping

Cave Diving

Logging

Big-Wave Surfing

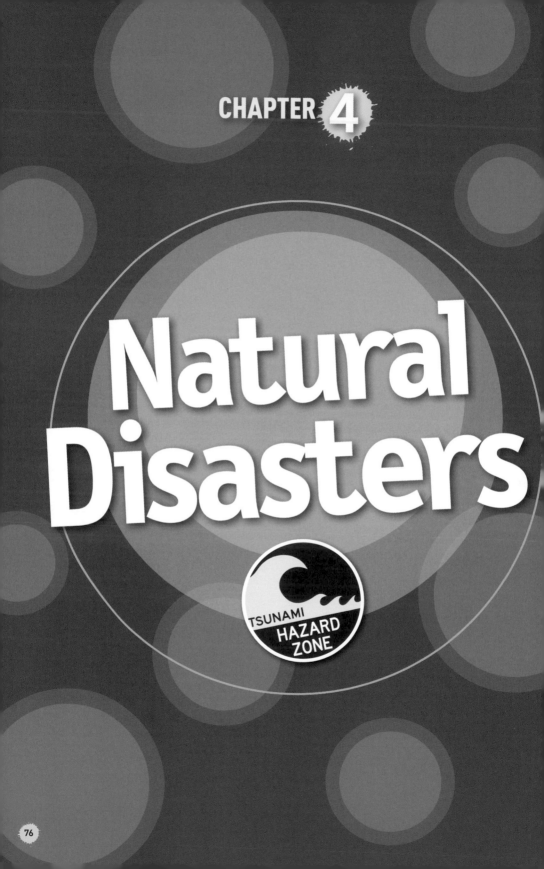

CHAPTER 4

Natural Disasters

TSUNAMI HAZARD ZONE

THE SKY DARKENS. WAVES CRASH. LIGHTNING FLASHES. THUNDER RUMBLES. The ground trembles beneath your feet. Buildings sway. Looks like a bad day for a picnic. What on Earth is going on out there? When the weather gets wild and the world gets wobbly, tragedy isn't far behind. Prepare to face the full force of Mother Nature's mean side—from flash floods to lava flows, earthquakes to hurricanes, lightning strikes to tsunamis—in this chapter that will have you running for cover.

Zzzaaap!

Shocking facts
about lightning ...

KRAAACK! **A thunderclap makes your heart race and sends Spot sprinting under the bed. But although thunder might set your nerves on edge, it's nothing more than an annoying racket—the aftereffect of a much more dangerous force of nature: lightning. Ground yourself for a breakdown of these bolts from above, which strike somewhere on Earth about 100 times every second ...**

STORM SURGE
Lightning gets its start in a storm cloud, where drops of rain and bits of ice blow and fall, bumping against each other to create static electricity (similar to the charge you create by rubbing your socked feet against the carpet). Positively charged particles rise to the cloud's top while negatively charged particles sink to the lower levels.

BATTERY UP
Ever notice how most batteries have little plus symbols (+) on their tops and minus symbols (-) on their bottoms? At this point the storm cloud is like a big fluffy battery—the most powerful battery on Earth. The difference between the positive and negative particles builds up a current, which arcs through the air as intracloud lightning, the most common type of lightning.

FOLLOW THE LEADER
More dangerous cloud-to-ground lightning works its way downward from the negatively charged lower levels of a cloud (or, in some cases, from the positively charged tippy top) through a stepped leader, a series of negative charges. The trip down the steps happens faster than the blink of an eye: around 200,000 miles an hour (300,000 km/h).

CONTACT!
Once the stepped leader gets within 150 feet (46 m) or so of the surface, it connects with a positive jolt of electricity that rises through an object on the ground, such as a tree, tower, building, or even you (never stand outside during a storm). This upward surge is called a streamer, and it's the flash of lightning you see with your eyes. When it connects with the leader, it creates a channel to conduct electricity from the earth to the cloud. *Zzzzt! Kraaack!*

BIG BOOM A bolt of lightning can be five times hotter than the surface of the sun. This superheat wreaks havoc with the surrounding air, creating a shock wave that we hear as thunder. You can tell how many miles you are from a lightning strike by counting the seconds between the flash and the peal of thunder, then dividing that number by five.

SOAR WINNERS Airplanes flying through storm clouds occasionally get struck by intracloud lightning. Don't fear flying in unfriendly skies, however; modern planes are designed to withstand multiple hits and keep on flying.

DOUBLE TROUBLE The old saying "lightning never strikes twice" is a sham. Bolts strike skyscrapers and other tall buildings twice, thrice, or more. New York City's Empire State Building gets zapped about 100 times each year.

ZAP CAPITAL The most likely time and place to get jolted by lightning in the United States is in the state of Florida on a Sunday afternoon (when the most people are typically outside enjoying the weekend). With its warm, stormy climate, Florida has twice as many deaths and injuries from lightning strikes as any other state.

UNLUCKY STRIKE Lightning strikes about 2,000 people worldwide each year, and nine out of every ten victims survive with symptoms ranging from memory loss to dizziness to bizarre scars. The odds of getting zapped for the average American are one in 5,000.

CHARGED UP Lightning can carry up to a billion volts of electricity, about 50,000 times the current of a typical industrial electrical accident.

TIM
THE GRIM REAPER'S
FATAL FACTS

You think lightning on Earth is scary? The upper atmosphere of Saturn is home to electrical storms the size of the United States, coursing with lightning a thousand times more powerful than Earth's.

AFTERSHOCK!

An interview with a lightning-strike survivor ...

One second Michele Young-Stone was standing in her parent's driveway. The next, she was lying on the ground ten feet [3 m] away. She'd been struck by lightning! Young-Stone was just 11 when she got zapped by this bolt from the blue. Not only did she survive the experience—it inspired her novel *The Handbook for Lightning Strike Survivors*, about a girl named Becca who is struck by lightning and no one believes her. Tim the Grim Reaper caught up with Young-Stone to find out if the truth was stranger than her fiction ...

TIM: What do you remember about the lightning strike?

YOUNG-STONE: I was in my parents' driveway in Chester, Virginia [U.S.A.], beneath a white sky, with no indication of a storm to come. My mom and I were getting ready to drive to the mall, which was about 20 miles [32 km] away. I was holding onto my dad's truck, about to climb in, when I was struck. I never saw it coming. Everything turned white; it was like falling into nothingness, and it was the loudest noise I've ever heard.

TIM: Do you feel unlucky that you were struck by lightning, or lucky that you were struck and survived?

YOUNG-STONE: I feel lucky that I was struck and survived. I wouldn't be the person I am if I hadn't been struck. My life has been filled with strange occurrences; I think the lightning strike is just part of who I am. I was a little "goth" in high school [a style that involves dressing in dark clothing and wearing moody makeup], and my dad said that it was because I was struck by lightning. My weirdness eventually made him a believer.

TIM: Did people doubt that you were struck, like with your character Becca?

YOUNG-STONE: My mom saw me get struck. Doing research for my novel, I learned that it's very common for both nearby observers and the victim to be in shock. We were both in shock. My mother may have also been affected by the electricity. Here's the kicker: After I got up off the ground, we did not speak. We climbed in my dad's truck, and we drove the 20 miles, silently, to the mall. On the way, it started to rain. When we got there, we finally spoke. My mom said, "You got struck by lightning." I said, "I got struck by lightning." We repeated the same things over and over and then drove home. My mother is a registered nurse, but we never went to the hospital. The whole experience was surreal and otherworldly. When we got home, we told my dad what happened. He made light of it. "If you'd been struck by lightning," he said, "you'd be dead." Not the case.

TIM: Some people think a lightning strike can grant superpowers. Any you'd like to share? Can you, say, heat a burrito without a microwave or change TV channels without the remote?

YOUNG-STONE: Of course—all those things! I don't really know. I can feel a storm coming. The hair on my arms stands up. I can sense when lightning will strike. It's a sensation from the gut … I sometimes feel like the lightning is "after me" in a way. I believe that once you've been struck, you're an easy pathway for the lightning. Scientists say this isn't true, but based on my research, once you've been struck, you're far more likely to be struck again. Lightning always takes the path of least resistance.

TIM: Lightning-strike victims can suffer from all sorts of symptoms—short-term memory loss, bizarre scars, dizziness, etc.—long after the strike. Did you deal with anything weird like that?

YOUNG-STONE: Yes! I have circulatory problems. I have Raynauld's disease, which means a shortage of blood to my appendages, including my ears, fingers, and toes. They are cold, sometimes numb, sometimes painful. My legs are purple during the winter. Also, for no reason, blood vessels burst in my fingers. I also remember very little about the actual event, except for the noise and the whiteness. For a long time, my electromagnetic field was altered. I couldn't wear a watch. It would not keep time, like in my novel.

TIM
THE GRIM REAPER'S
FATAL FACTS

Depending on your point of view, Roy Sullivan was either the luckiest or unluckiest person who ever lived. The former U.S. park ranger was struck by lightning seven times throughout his life. He died of unrelated causes in 1983.

Rattle and Roll
EARTHQUAKES

ONE SPRING EVENING IN 1964, THE EARTH IN ANCHORAGE, ALASKA, U.S.A., SPLIT OPEN, DEVOURING BUILDINGS AND RIPPING CHASMS IN THE STREETS. Earthquake! The "temblor" lasted for less than five minutes. But for the people caught in it, stumbling for shelter on ground that pitched like ocean waves, the world seemed to wobble for hours. When the shaking stopped, more than a dozen were dead. Sparks showered from downed power lines. Geysers of flame shot from twisted gas lines. Houses were reduced to rubble.

The nightmare was far from over. Soon, walls of water called tsunamis washed away villages and claimed more than a hundred additional lives, some as far away as California. The Great Alaskan Earthquake literally changed the landscape of the state (some areas were raised as much as four stories; others dropped below the high-tide mark). And it wasn't even the most powerful earthquake in recorded history. It was also far from the deadliest.

The ground beneath your feet might feel as solid as a rock, but it's actually moving every minute of every hour of every day. Earth's crust is broken into plates that fit together like puzzle pieces. They're always on the march, a phenomenon known as continental drift. (The plates creep about as fast as your fingernails grow.) As they move, the plates grind against each other along fractures in the crust known as faults, gradually releasing pressure during thousands of tiny quakes per day. But when pressure builds between plates over decades or centuries, the plates can slip and release devastating seismic waves that race through rock, sand, and soil like ripples in a pond. This sudden burst of energy is what causes the most powerful quakes.

The worst quakes—called "megathrust" earthquakes—happen when one plate is forced underneath another, creating a tremendous buildup of pressure. (The Great Alaskan Earthquake of 1964 was one such earthquake.) Such a sudden release of seismic energy can have far-reaching effects.

Alaska's earthquake sunk boats as far away as Louisiana. All powerful earthquakes can cause landslides, fires, structural damage to cities and roads, and unstoppable tsunamis. A 16th-century quake in China, the deadliest ever recorded, claimed the lives of more than 800,000 people.

A type of turf known as bedrock is more stable in an earthquake's seismic waves. Sandy ground is the opposite. It succumbs to a phenomenon known as liquefaction in which the soil becomes a sort of sand soup unable to support the buildings and roads above it.

Geologists measure the energy released by earthquakes on the moment magnitude scale, which measures the total energy released by quakes. Each number on the scale represents ten times more shaking power than the number below it. (A magnitude 7 earthquake, for example, is ten times more powerful than a magnitude 6 quake.) Here's a breakdown of the shake-measuring system ...

8.9

9–10: EXTREME
Feels like the end of the world
The Great Alaskan Earthquake measured 9.2. The strongest earthquake ever recorded rocked Chile in 1960. As many as 6,000 died in the quake and the resulting tsunamis.

Death tolls rise when quakes strike cities that aren't built for a beating. As many as 3,000 people died— mostly from collapsing buildings— when a massive earthquake struck San Francisco, California, U.S.A., in 1906. Today, the City by the Bay's structures have been reinforced to survive earthquakes.

8

7–8: MAJOR
Feels like the ground is a raging ocean
Earthquakes of magnitude 8 hit about once a year somewhere on Earth. They're capable of widespread damage.

7

5–6: MODERATE
Feels like the world is swaying
Quakes on the upper end can do major damage in unprepared cities. A 6.6 quake killed more than 20,000 people in Iran in 2003.

6 5

-1 0 1 2 3 4

1–4: LIGHT
Feels like a truck driving by
Most quakes fall within this range.

An earthquake is only the beginning. Large quakes are often followed by powerful aftershocks that can interfere with rescue efforts.

TIM
THE GRIM REAPER'S
FATAL FACTS

Scientists can predict hurricanes and other natural disasters. Why not earthquakes? Although most temblors occur 50 miles (80 km) or less below the Earth's surface, they're just too many—and they happen too randomly—for geologists to predict.

Volcanoes

Menacing Mountains

MORE THAN HALF A MILLION PEOPLE LIVE NEXT TO A SLEEPING GIANT THE SIZE OF A MOUNTAIN IN NAPLES, ITALY, AND NO ONE KNOWS WHEN IT WILL WAKE UP. This beast has a name: Mount Vesuvius. It's one of the world's most famous volcanoes, and it has a deadly history. Around lunchtime on August 4 in A.D. 79, the mountain erupted, belching a column of ash, boiling mud, and pumice pebbles 20 miles (32 km) into the air. When it fell to earth over the course of the day, the debris buried the nearby Roman cities of Pompeii and Herculaneum in up to 20 feet (6 m) of ash and stone. An estimated 16,000 people perished. The towns were wiped from history until they were rediscovered more than 1,500 years later.

Mount Vesuvius is one of nearly 2,000 volcanoes in the world that are considered active, or have the potential to erupt. Earth's crust rides on massive plates floating on a sea of molten rock called magma, which bubbles to the surface wherever two plates meet. Volcanoes work like pressure valves for this magma (known as lava when it reaches the surface). In effusive volcanoes (such as the famous volcanoes of Hawaii, U.S.A.), the lava flows at a steady rate, often forming new mountains and islands. Volcanoes with a lot of gases dissolved in their magma and a high content of a chemical known as silica have explosive eruptions in which they literally blow their tops. Potentially much deadlier than effusive eruptions, explosive volcanoes vaporize the landscape in every direction with hot gas and carpet the terrain with choking ash. Mount Vesuvius's eruption in A.D. 79 was an explosive one.

The mountain is far from dormant; it has erupted about 50 times since it destroyed Pompeii and Herculaneum. Today, 600,000 people live in the mountain's "red zone," an area that could be destroyed should Vesuvius blow its top again. Geologists are certain that it will. Fortunately, volcanoes usually show symptoms (such as earthquakes and changes in groundwater) before they erupt. When the ground begins to quiver in the shadow of Vesuvius, residents know what to do: leave or lose their lives like the people of Pompeii.

Most earthquakes lie along plate boundaries in the so-called Ring of Fire, a 25,000-mile (40,000-km) horseshoe-shaped string of volcanoes around the edges of the Pacific Ocean.

Volcanic Hazards

TOXIC VOG
Risk: Low
Along with ash, volcanoes vent sulfur dioxide into the air, creating a volcanic fog (called vog) that can lead to breathing problems and burning eyes.

LAVA FLOWS
Risk: Low
The magma that flows from a volcano's fissures can reach 2,000 degrees Fahrenheit (1093°C)—hot enough to melt anything in its path (including people). Fortunately, lava flows slowly and is easy to outrun (think of lava as the zombie of natural hazards).

EARTHQUAKES
Risk: Medium
Volcanic eruptions are preceded by temblors, which bring their own assortment of dangers: landslides, structural damage, and tsunamis.

BLANKETING ASH AND DEBRIS
Risk: High
Explosive volcanoes launch thousands of tons of ash, mud, and rock high into the atmosphere. The debris can bury entire towns. Massive eruptions can spew enough ash into the atmosphere to envelope the entire planet, blocking the sun and causing a "volcanic winter."

PYROCLASTIC FLOWS
Risk: Extreme
Mount Vesuvius's most famous victims were roasted in an avalanche of ash and gas that hurtled down the volcano's sides at hundreds of miles an hour. Such pyroclastic flows can reach more than 1,000 degrees Fahrenheit (538°C) in the blink of an eye. Plaster casts made of the victims showed they likely died too quickly to feel pain.

TIM
THE GRIM REAPER'S
FATAL FACTS

The geyser-riddled Yellowstone National Park in Wyoming, U.S.A., sits above a "supervolcano" that last blew its top 640,000 years ago.

EVIL EYES
HURRICANES

EYEWALL:
The clouds that spiral around the eye are home to the most damaging and intense winds and rain.

EYE:
This circle of low pressure, which can sprawl for 20 to 40 miles (32 to 64 km), forms the center of the hurricane. It's eerily calm, a region of blue skies and starry nights. People caught in the eye might be fooled into thinking the storm has passed. It's a potentially deadly mistake.

RIDING LOW IN THE WATER, THEIR HOLDS LADEN WITH GOLD AND SILVER WORTH $300 MILLION IN TODAY'S U.S. DOLLARS, SPANISH TREASURE SHIPS CALLED GALLEONS SET SAIL FOR HOME FROM CUBA ON JULY 25, 1715. The galleons were part of the world's most powerful navy, heavily armed against the pirates prowling the Caribbean. But cannons were useless against the monster that bore down on the treasure fleet a week later off the coast of Florida. Furious gales ripped apart the rigging. Two-story waves smashed the ships to splinters. One by one, the galleons succumbed to a storm that seemed endless. Of the eleven ships that set out, only one made it home. Sunken treasure littered beaches across the Atlantic coast of Florida. More than a thousand sailors lost their lives.

It's no wonder the Spanish called the storm that sank their fleet a *huracan*, the Maya word for an evil weather god. Today, meteorologists can predict and track hurricanes, known as typhoons when they develop in the western Pacific and cyclones when they form in the northern Indian Ocean. People living in the storm's path see it coming. They have time to evacuate to safer areas, making these monster storms less deadly than in the days of the Spanish treasure fleet. Still, hurricanes cause tremendous damage and, yes, even death.

Hurricanes need the right combination of warm seas, moist air, and strong winds to

RAIN BANDS:

These pinwheeling bands of storm clouds form the fringes of a hurricane. They can unleash torrential rain and tornadoes once they reach land, but the worst weather is yet to come ...

The conditions for hurricane formation are more favorable during certain times of the year. In the Atlantic, Gulf of Mexico, Caribbean, and central Pacific, hurricane season runs from June 1 to November 30. Eastern Pacific hurricanes are more common from May 15 to November 30.

SIZING UP THE STORM

Hurricane strength is rated on the Saffir/Simpson scale, which divides storms into five categories ...

CATEGORY 1
Wind speed: 74–95 miles an hour (119–153 km/h)
This is the lowest rating a storm can have and still be declared a hurricane. Category 1 hurricanes can cause mild damage and some flooding along the coasts.

CATEGORY 2
Wind speed: 96–110 miles an hour (154–177 km/h)
Category 2 storms can damage roofs and rip boats from their moorings.

CATEGORY 3
Wind speed: 111–130 miles an hour (178–209 km/h)
Storm surge can damage houses and structures inland. Strong winds can damage roofs and break windows.

CATEGORY 4
Wind speed: 131–155 miles an hour (210–249 km/h)
Winds this strong can tear the roofs off houses and cause flooding far from shore. Storm surge can wash the unwary out to sea.

CATEGORY 5
Wind speed: above 155 miles an hour (249 km/h)
The deadliest and most damaging type of hurricane. These storms are monsters, capable of knocking over houses and causing massive flooding.

form. This is why they typically take shape over tropical oceans and coasts, where the warm ocean waters create an area of low pressure in the moist air. The movement of air from areas of high pressure to low pressure is what creates wind. Bundles of thunderstorms form, fueled by the warm ocean temps and whipped into a swirling shape by the Earth's rotation and growing wind. What starts as a tropical depression becomes a tropical storm (and is given a name) when the winds reach 39 miles an hour (63 km/h). When the winds top 74 miles an hour (119 km/h), the storm is officially declared a hurricane. Fortunately, hurricanes aren't common. Only about 10 percent of the tropical disturbances that form each year

develop into full-fledged hurricanes. And because they rely on warm, moist air from the sea to sustain them, hurricanes usually weaken and die as soon as they make landfall.

The power of these superstorms is both awesome and terrifying. Hurricane winds can exceed 155 miles an hour (249 km/h), tearing apart houses and tossing cars. When they hit land, hurricanes bring flooding rain and sometimes spawn tornadoes. Even if a hurricane never makes landfall, its wind can create massive waves three stories high that crash ashore as deadly storm surge. In the United States each year, these storms cause an average of $10 billion dollars in damage— more than 30 times the value of the treasure spilled by the Spanish fleet.

SAVAGE SWELLS

These gnarly waves will ruin any day at the beach

TSUNAMIS

A tsunami racing across the deep sea doesn't look very scary. It's little more than a series of knee-high swells. But when one of these killer waves slams into land, you better head for higher ground. A tsunami is one of the deadliest forces on Earth.

Tsunamis are spawned by coastal or undersea earthquakes, submerged landslides, volcanic eruptions, or even asteroid impacts. These events displace ocean water around or above them, triggering rolling waves that zoom across the ocean at the speed of a jet airplane—fast enough to cross the entire Pacific Ocean (where tsunamis are most common) in less than a day. When these energy-packed waves reach shallow waters, they undergo a terrifying transformation. The low point of a tsunami wave—called its trough—reaches shore first, causing waters on beaches and harbors to retreat and expose the sea floor. Coastal residents who recognize this warning sign know it's time to race inland and seek the high ground. Within five minutes, a wall of water as high as 100 feet (30 m) sloshes ashore and rages over the land, washing away entire towns.

Tsunamis often kill more people than the quakes that caused them. A 2011 earthquake off the coast of Japan unleashed a devastating tsunami with waves topping 20 feet (6 m). Nearly 15,000 people perished. A 9.15-magnitude quake in the Indian Ocean in 2004 spawned a tsunami that killed more than 200,000 people, making it the most lethal tsunami in recorded history. A network of sensors monitor for tsunamis in the Pacific Ocean, giving people some warning to climb for safety should one of these killer waves head their way.

TSUNAMIS VS. TIDAL WAVES

People often mistakenly call tsunamis "tidal waves," but tsunamis and tidal waves are nothing alike. Tidal waves are predictable surges of water up rivers and into narrow bays against the current. They're caused by the gravitational tug of the moon (and to a lesser extent the sun and planets). They're not nearly as dangerous (or as unpredictable) as tsunamis.

RIP CURRENTS

Like a wave in reverse, these strong currents flow from the beach back into the open ocean, potentially dragging unsuspecting swimmers out to sea. Rip currents (often incorrectly called riptides) can form on any beach with breaking waves—even tiny ones. Waves striking the beach carry a tremendous amount of water, and all that water needs to return to the ocean. When the water drains through a channel in the beach bottom or a sandbar or reef off the beach, a rip current forms.

These currents travel up to five miles an hour (8 km/h)—fast enough to overpower most swimmers. Rip-current victims compare the experience to swimming on a treadmill. No matter how frantically they paddle and kick, they can't outswim the current.

Eventually, they tire and get sucked into the ocean. Rip currents are responsible for nearly 50 deaths each year on beaches in the United States.

Escaping the grip of a rip current is easy if you keep a level head. Most of these currents are less than 30 feet (9 m) wide. If you calmly swim sideways, parallel to the beach rather than against the current, you'll eventually move out of the rip and can return to the beach. Some rip currents are easy to spot by looking for streaks of churned-up sand coursing out to sea. It's always smart to ask a lifeguard for the location of any rip currents before jumping in. When in doubt, stay out of the water.

RIP CURRENTS VS. UNDERTOWS

Rip currents are often mistakenly called undertows, but undertows are a different kind of current. Instead of flowing away from shore on the surface like a rip, undertows run along the ocean floor. Most breaking waves create a slight undertow that you can feel pulling on your feet as seawater sloshes off the beach. Powerful undertows created by large waves can suck beachgoers beneath the surface.

FREAK WAVES

It's not shipwrecking sea monsters or circling sharks that lurk in the nightmares of seasoned sailors. Old salts dread a different breed of beast: an avalanche of seawater that wallops boats in the calmest of seas. These monsters were considered just another sailing legend until an 85-foot (26-m) specimen struck an oil rig in the North Sea off Norway in 1995. Now they have a name: rogue waves. Also known as a freak wave, a rogue wave is any mountain of water that rears up to twice the height of nearby waves—although they often grow much mightier. Three 10-story waves pounded the cruise ship *Norwegian Dawn* in 2005, smashing windows, flooding several decks, and injuring four passengers.

Scientists know that waves are created by wind blowing over a body of water. Those tube-shaped "barrels" that surfers ride off the north shore of Hawaii? They started thousands of miles away as ripples blown across the sea's surface. The origin of rogue waves, however, remains a mystery. Scientists suspect they form when multiple normal waves combine to form a supersize wave. Strong ocean currents can also focus and magnify a wave into a towering wall of water powerful enough to scuttle even the sturdiest ships. Whatever the cause, these legendary waves are more common than scientists once thought. Satellite imagery revealed ten of these monsters prowling the ocean in one three-week period.

SNEAKER WAVES

Also known as sleeper waves, these unpredictable and dangerous swells are rogue waves that reach the beach. They're abnormally large and often catch beachgoers by surprise, sometimes sweeping them out to sea. A sleeper wave washed five people into the ocean in 2009 at Acadia National Park in Maine, U.S.A. The lesson here: Never turn your back on the ocean.

TIM
THE GRIM REAPER'S
FATAL FACTS

Rogue waves can form in any large body of water—even lakes. Scientists suspect that a rogue wave may have sunk the cargo ship *Edmund Fitzgerald* in Lake Superior in 1975.

TWISTER TALES

TERRIFYING FACTS ABOUT TORNADOES

They spin. They create tremendous wind. They leave death and destruction in their paths. In many ways, tornadoes are like the meaner children of hurricanes. (In fact, hurricanes can even spawn tornadoes.) But while tornadoes are much smaller than hurricanes, they're faster, stronger, more unpredictable, and often deadlier. Nearly twice as many people have died in tornadoes than hurricanes in the United States since 1940. Here are 10 facts about these terrifying twisters ...

1 The safest place to be during a tornado is underground in a fortified tornado shelter. If one isn't available, take cover in a bathtub or beneath a door frame.

2 Tornado winds can exceed 300 miles an hour (480 km/h)—more than strong enough to toss cars through the air.

3 Twisters occur most frequently in Tornado Alley, a stretch of the United States from the Midwest to the South. An average of 1,000 tornadoes touch down in the United States each year.

4 People who have survived close calls with tornadoes say they sound like a freight train screaming just inches past their ears.

5 Tornadoes spawn from a supercell: a rotating thunderstorm that forms when areas of low pressure (hot air) and high pressure (cold air) collide to form a spinning funnel-shaped cloud that stretches from the ground to the storm clouds.

6 When a tornado forms over water, it's known as a tornadic waterspout.

7 The most powerful tornado on record, known as the Tri-State Tornado, killed 695 people and injured 2,027 when it tore a 300-mile (483-km) path of destruction through Missouri, Indiana, and Illinois, U.S.A., in the spring of 1925. Its winds topped 260 miles an hour (418 km/h).

8 Tornadoes are difficult to study. Unlike hurricanes, they can't be forecasted or tracked with accuracy, and they're so powerful that they destroy scientific instruments. Consequently, scientists still aren't certain what causes a tornado to form.

9 Hurricanes can travel thousands of miles but they're limited to the tropics. Tornadoes typically only travel for about ten minutes, but they can form all over the world.

TORNADO TYPES

Like hurricanes, tornadoes are ranked according to strength on a scale of 1 to 5. Per the enhanced Fujita scale ...

EF1 TORNADO
Wind speed: 86–110 miles an hour (138–177 km/h)

The weakest tornadoes are still strong enough to peel the roofs off houses and push your car on the road.

EF2 TORNADO
Wind speed: 111–135 miles an hour (178–217 km/h)

EF2 twisters can smash mobile homes and snap trees in half.

EF3 TORNADO
Wind speed: 136–165 miles an hour (218–266 km/h)

Even the strongest houses can't stand up to these twisters, which are powerful enough to toss cars and overturn trains.

EF4 TORNADO
Wind speed: 166–200 miles an hour (267–322 km/h)

More powerful than the strongest hurricanes, EF4 tornadoes can level entire blocks and rip large trees from the ground, turning them into deadly missiles.

EF5 TORNADO
Wind speed: Above 200 miles an hour (above 322 km/h)

The most powerful tornadoes cause unbelievable—even bizarre—damage (such as ripping grass from the ground and stripping the bark off trees). EF5 twisters have tossed cars farther than the length of a football field.

Deadly
Oddities

Freaky and furious forces of nature ...

HOLE TRUTH

Imagine if the ground beneath your house suddenly opened up and swallowed your entire bedroom—including your bed with you in it. That's exactly what happened when a sinkhole formed beneath a home near Tampa, Florida, U.S.A. Sinkholes open when the acid in rainwater eats away at a foundation of soft rock (such as limestone or pumice) beneath the soil. The dissolved rock leaves an underground hole that collapses underneath the weight of whatever lies above, such as houses or roads. A sinkhole in Guatemala swallowed a three-story building.

HELMET WEATHER

Thunk! Thunk! Thunk! When hailstones fall from the heavens, look out below! These frozen balls of water can grow to the size of a baseball and strike the ground at more than 100 miles an hour (160 km/h), damaging cars, breaking windows, and killing animals and people. Hundreds perished in a massive hailstorm that struck the Himalaya a thousand years ago. Hail forms in large clouds where droplets of frozen water are held aloft by strong winds until they grow so heavy that they plunge to the earth.

ROAD HAZARD

You might think hailstones are the same as frozen raindrops, but freezing rain is a different phenomenon that comes with its own dangers. When supercool rain hits a frozen surface—such as a road, tree limb, or power line—it freezes immediately, creating a sheet of ice. Highways covered with such "black ice" become dangerously slick, leading to car accidents. Tree limbs and power lines can snap under the intense weight of frozen rain.

GREAT BALLS OF FIRE

It comes into the world as a sizzling sphere of energy roughly the size of a human head. It makes its grand exit with a small explosion. Ball lightning is one of nature's freakiest special effects. These elusive orbs of fire dance over the ground and launch high into the sky. Eyewitnesses have confused these electrical spheres for everything from galloping ghosts to flying saucers. Scientists suspect that ball lightning sparks to life when normal lightning strikes the ground and ignites silicon, a chemical element in the soil. The silicon erupts in a fiery globe of burning oxygen that darts willy-nilly through the air.

LAVA LIGHT SHOW

Volcanic eruptions produce more than clouds of ash and rivers of scalding lava. Under the right conditions, a volcano can spawn what's called a "dirty thunderstorm": a frightening lightning display on par with the Catatumbo spectacle seen at the end of this chapter. Bits of ash and rock collide in the volcanic plume and generate hundreds of lightning flashes per hour.

TIM
THE GRIM REAPER'S
FATAL FACTS

Europeans in the 18th century tried to prevent hailstorms by firing cannons into clouds. (It didn't work.)

93

Avoiding earthquakes, volcanoes, hurricanes, and tornadoes is easy: Stay out of their danger zones. Dodging wildfires and floods ... not so much. Of all the natural disasters, these two are

Wildfires

Hell's Gales

If you thought a tornado was terrifying, imagine a twister made of flame scorching everything in its path! Such "fire devils" (aka "fire whirls" and "firenadoes") are real, and they form when wildfires slurp all the oxygen from the air, creating vortexes of wind as fresh air rushes in and upward (hot air rises). Temperatures inside a firenado can reach 2,000 degrees Fahrenheit (1093°C), hot enough to ignite nearby trees and anyone who gets too close. Fortunately, fire whirls move slowly, but they can grow to 50 feet (15 m) wide and the height of a normal tornado.

When droughts or dry weather turn lush forests brown and brittle, the forecast calls for fire. All it takes is a spark from a bolt of lightning or car backfire or even the heat of the sun to ignite an inferno that consumes everything—trees, homes, and even people—in its path. Even scarier: Wildfires can travel as fast as a human can run.

An average of 100,000 wildfires devour up to 5 million acres (2 million ha) of forest in the United States every year. Although most of these infernos have man-made causes—out-of-control campfires or deliberately set blazes—the dry underbrush and winds that fuel them are nature's doing. The number of wildfires is increasing worldwide as temperatures climb and droughts draw on, side effects of climate change.

While these blazes can start anywhere, they're most common in the western United States. Here, heat, drought, dry winds, and frequent thunderstorms create the perfect conditions for runaway firestorms. But while these blazes destroy property and cost human lives—often the brave firefighters sent to fight them—they at least have some benefits. Wildfires consume dead underbrush, clearing the land and returning nutrients to the soil for a new crop of forest.

the most widespread. They happen all over the world! Wildfires and floods also arise from almost completely opposite conditions. **But which is deadlier? See for yourself ...**

VS. *Floods*

If you ever forgot you left the water running while filling the bathtub, you have an inkling of how fast a flood can get out of control. Also known as a deluge, a flood is the result of any runaway rise in waters on normally dry land. Floods occur across the world, even in deserts. If you live near a coast or a river—or even a creek—you might face a flood someday.

The most common floods occur when rivers or streams overflow, usually because of heavy rains or the rapid melting of ice in mountains upstream. Even a badly placed beaver dam can cause a river to jump its banks. Hurricanes can also cause massive flooding. Nearly 2,000 people died when Hurricane Katrina, a category 5 hurricane, caused levees (walls built to keep out floodwaters) to fail around New Orleans, Louisiana, U.S.A.

The most destructive deluges are called hundred-year floods, so named because they're rare (although they're becoming more common because of climate change). Rushing water is one of Earth's most powerful forces. Large floods can wash away the foundations beneath homes and the pilings that support bridges. Flash floods—which happen quickly in areas prone to flooding—are doubly dangerous because they strike with little warning.

The ordeal isn't over when the waters recede. Floods leave behind thick layers of mud, pesticides, and other toxic chemicals and debris. Contaminated drinking water combined with power outages make for an uncomfortable recovery in areas that were recently underwater.

Island Homes

Little can be done to protect property from the awesome power of rushing, rising water in a flood, but that didn't stop inventive farmers from trying to save their houses when a tributary of the Mississippi River jumped its banks in 2011. Using construction equipment, they built levees from sandbags around their homes to keep the rising waters at bay.

THREE SUPER-STORMS

MOUNT DOOM

Geologists measure the might of volcanic eruptions on a scale of 0 to 7: the volcanic explosivity index. The 1815 eruption of Mount Tambora on the island of Sumbawa in Indonesia measured a 7—the most powerful ever recorded. The initial eruption obliterated the top third of the mountain, creating a shockwave that was heard up to 1,200 miles (2,000 km) away. Distant ship captains thought they were hearing the cannons of a sea battle. The volcano spewed ash into the atmosphere for the next three years, lowering global temperatures. Crops across the world withered. As many as 90,000 people perished as a result of the eruption.

TITANIC TYPHOON

The largest hurricane ever recorded churned across the western Pacific Ocean in October 1979, growing in power and size until it maxed out at 1,380 miles (2,220 km) in diameter, larger than half the contiguous United States. Named Typhoon Tip, the superstorm's gusts topped 190 miles an hour (306 km/h). Although Tip had lost some steam before it made landfall in southern Japan, the storm still claimed 86 lives.

SURGE STORM

The largest electrical storm on Earth ignites the sky for more than half the year in Venezuela, where the Catatumbo River empties into Lake Maracaibo. Called Catatumbo lightning, the storm has raged for centuries, serving as a beacon for sailors who know not to steer too close. As many as 300 bolts strike each hour. A combination of factors—warm equatorial waters, moisture-laden trade winds, and methane produced by swamps and oil deposits—turn the skies above the region into the perfect lightning generator.

THE *Big* ONES

SUDDEN DEATH

RUN FOR YOUR LIFE!

DANGER ZONE

RISKY BUSINESS

Tsunamis

Earthquakes

Volcanoes

Hurricanes

Lightning Strikes

Wildfires

KILL-O-METER

GRIM OUTDOORS

TIM
THE GRIM REAPER
RANKS NATURAL DISASTERS

CHAPTER 5

Man-Made and Menacing

SMARTPHONES, SMART CARS, SMART TOASTERS—gadgets are becoming more complicated while promising to simplify your life. But sometimes technology can ruin lives instead of improving them. Take a break from your tech and tear into this chapter on weird weaponry, major malfunctions, dangerous toys, and false starts of the state of the art.

GAME OVER

How VIDEO GAMES take their toll on your real-life health meter ...

IF YOU'VE EVER STAYED UP UNTIL THE WEE HOURS, HUNCHED AND BLEARY-EYED IN FRONT OF YOUR GAME SYSTEM TRYING TO FINISH JUST ONE MORE LEVEL, CONSIDER THIS A CAUTIONARY TALE: In 2005, a young man actually died from a marathon gaming session. He lived in South Korea, where gaming tournaments are televised like sporting events and the best players become highly paid celebrities. Online gaming is especially popular. More than 30 percent of South Koreans have online-gaming accounts.

And so the stage was set for one man's final mission with the strategy game *StarCraft*. The 28-year-old player slouched over his laptop in an Internet café binge-playing for 50 hours, hitting "pause" only for catnaps and bathroom breaks. According to witnesses, he barely ate or drank. Eventually, the man collapsed and was rushed to the hospital. Doctors couldn't revive him. He died of heart failure from extreme exhaustion.

Believe it or not, this expired player wasn't the first fatal victim of "video game addiction," or the inability to put down the controller. Binge-playing has doomed gamers as far back as the heyday of arcades in the 1980s. And while studies show that gaming in small doses—less than an hour each day—can be good for you (improving hand-eye coordination, boosting creativity, and increasing general happiness), too much game time can have the opposite effect. In video games you get multiple lives; in the real world you get only one.

WHEN CONTRAPTIONS ATTACK ...

KILLER CAR

The 1971 Ford Pinto is infamous for one fatal design flaw: It could explode when struck from behind by another car. Pinto fires claimed the lives of 27 drivers, resulting in a recall of the car by the manufacturer.

PHONE-BATTERY BLASTS

Reports began surfacing in 2003 of cell phones exploding if their owners tried to take a call while the phone was charging. It turns out that bootleg batteries—counterfeit replacements for the original batteries—were to blame.

THE FINAL HOUR

History's oddest account of "murder by mechanism" comes from the book *The Burglar Caught by a Skeleton* by Jeremy Clay, in which the author cites an 1876 police report of a man killed inside the clockwork of a church tower in what is now Poland. The victim, a tourist named Mr. Maybrook, was admiring the ornate automatons—primitive robots—that hammered the village's church bell each hour. When one of the bell bashers sprung into action to toll the time, the startled Maybrook leaped backward—directly into the strike zone of a second hammer-wielding automaton. For Mr. Maybrook, his time had come.

‹‹‹‹ NEST OF BEES
WIELDED IN 11TH-CENTURY A.D. CHINA

Facing one of these weapons on the battlefield would be like having a front-row seat to the world's worst fireworks finale. Invented in China, the birthplace of gunpowder, the nest of bees was an ornate box crammed with dozens of rocket-powered arrows. Soldiers would set several nests on the battlefield and fire them off simultaneously, sending hundreds of arrows soaring straight into the enemy's ranks. The weapon wasn't known for its accuracy—getting struck by an arrow was more a matter of bad luck—but it still filled enemy troops with terror.

UMBRELLA ››››
DART-GUN
WIELDED IN 20TH-CENTURY EUROPE

Like a gadget out of a James Bond film, this umbrella fired a BB-size pellet coated in a deadly poison, which only needed to break the skin to kill. A Bulgarian agent used such an umbrella to assassinate enemy-of-the-state Georgi Markov, who recalled being shot by such a device before falling ill and dying the next day.

HISTORY'S
WEiRDEST

<<<<

BOOMERANG
WIELDED IN 8TH-CENTURY B.C. AUSTRALIA AND ELSEWHERE

More than just uncanny flying objects, boomerangs are ancient hunting weapons, wielded for at least 10,000 years in Australia and even longer in other parts of the world. These hand-carved hunks of hardwood come in several varieties, including shaped sticks that soar straight (better for bonking animals in the head during a hunt) and the more famous returning type, which whizzes back to its thrower like a loyal Frisbee—provided it's thrown correctly. The secret of the boomerang's round-trip flight is its shape, which makes it curve through the air.

<<<<

LANTERN SHIELD
WIELDED IN 15TH-CENTURY A.D. ITALY

A shield with a secret weapon, this metal disc had a hook or internal cavity for carrying a lantern. Crafty sword fighters wielded this shield with one hand during duels in the dim hours of sunrise or sunset. They would hide the lantern until the last minute, then reveal it to bedazzle foes, making them easier to impale. See, sometimes a good defense is the best offense!

>>>>

SHURIKEN
WIELDED IN 16TH-CENTURY A.D. JAPAN

This blade-tipped metal disc—aka the throwing star—has become the ninja's calling card in karate movies, in which black-clad assassins whiz shurikens at foes with terrifying accuracy. In reality, throwing stars were used mainly to slow pursuers, but one lucky strike could still kill a foe.

WEAPONS

Playtime's OVER

Three TERRIBLE toys banned for being DEADLY ...

LAWN DARTS

YEAR BANNED: 1988

These backyard tossing toys—also called jarts—didn't look particularly deadly in the box. Each dart was a foot long (30 cm) and tipped with a blunted metal spike designed to puncture grass but not skin. Players took turns tossing the darts underhand toward circular targets laid on the lawn in a game designed as an alternative to horseshoes.

SOUNDS FUN. WHAT COULD GO WRONG?

Lawn Darts became deadly when you added two ingredients: altitude and gravity. Once tossed high into the air, the weighted darts plummeted to the ground spike-first with enough force to puncture skulls and injure eyes. Nearly 5,000 kids wound up in emergency rooms after getting hit by falling darts. The dangerous game was banned for sale in 1988. Today, even online-auction websites refuse to sell it.

DANGEROUS BUT NOT DEADLY ...

Feed Me

...mouth really moves!

CABBAGE PATCH SNACK TIME KID

This motorized doll simulated snacking on plastic potato chips and other artificial treats placed inside its mouth. There was just one problem: The motor-mouth didn't have an off switch. It just kept chewing and chewing until the doll swallowed the fake food. Kids whose long hair dangled too close to the doll's jaws had some painful playtimes.

FIRING STARFIGHTERS

YEAR BANNED: 1978

Toy spaceships based on the original *Battlestar Galactica* TV show shipped with tiny plastic torpedoes ready for launch. You simply loaded the missiles into the spring-powered firing mechanism, pressed the firing button, and—pop!—they shot across the room with surprising force.

SOUNDS FUN. WHAT COULD GO WRONG?

The ships' firing mechanisms had hair triggers, which led to accidental launches and eye injuries. This eventually caused a ban on all toys armed with working torpedoes.

FISHER-PRICE LITTLE PEOPLE

YEAR BANNED: NEVER, BUT REDESIGNED IN 1991

Action figures for small children, these colorful thumb-size dolls are little more than round plastic heads attached to tube-shaped torsos. They come in a variety of facial types and career uniforms and are compatible with a wide assortment of vehicles and play sets.

SOUNDS FUN. WHAT COULD GO WRONG?

Early versions of the Little People were a little too little. Small children could swallow the toys and choke. The toys were redesigned in 1991. Now they're too large to become choking hazards.

SLIP 'N SLIDE

How's this for a twist? The Slip 'N Slide—a long sheet of plastic that's slippery when wet—was declared dangerous only for adults and teenagers (whose heavier body weight can result in spinal injuries if they use the slide). That means you can scold your parents or older siblings if you catch them playing on it.

EASY-BAKE OVEN

This fake oven cooked real cakes using light bulbs as a heat source. Sounds sweet? It had a sour surprise. A cook's fingers could get caught in the oven's opening, which resulted in more than a dozen bad burns. The flaw was fixed in 2007.

SNACKS UNDER ATTACK

FOUR KILLER-CANDY MYTHS ... CRUSHED!

YOUR HALLOWEEN TREAT IS A DEADLY TRICK!

THE MYTH: On a night devoted to frights, it's the most terrifying scenario of all: Your haul of Halloween sweets might be laced with pins and poisons! Warnings of toxic Halloween treats—tainted by some grouchy neighbor or modern-day witch fed up with kids traipsing across the lawn—are repeated every year and lent credibility by local hospitals and fire stations offering to x-ray candy apples and Tootsie Rolls for razor blades and other nasty surprises.

THE TRUTH: Tales of deadly tricks played on Halloween treats go back to before the 1970s, but genuine reports of candy poisoning are both rare and blown out of proportion. That doesn't mean you shouldn't be wary of unsealed candy from neighbors you barely know, but ultimately the scariest part of Halloween should always be your costume, not your candy.

LIFE SAVERS CANDIES HAVE HOLES TO PREVENT CHOKING!

THE MYTH: It's a sweet ending to a sad beginning: After his daughter choked on a piece of hard candy, a heartbroken inventor created a round mint with a hole in the middle. The whole point of the hole was so people could still breathe through the candy if they accidentally inhaled it. The inventor named his candy Life Savers, hoping it would spare other children from the same fate as his daughter.

THE TRUTH: Life Savers creator Clarence Crane—a candy maker from Ohio, U.S.A.—never had a daughter who choked on candy. When he invented Life Savers in 1912, they came in one color and flavor: white peppermint. Crane added the hole to give his mint the appearance of a tiny life preserver—which is why he called his creation Life Savers. The treat was never intended as a safer alternative to hard candy. Like any small piece of food, it's even possible to choke on a Life Saver, so savor with caution!

BUBBLE YUM IS MADE OF SPIDER EGGS!

THE MYTH: You might think it's ho-hum today, but soft bubble gum was a breakthrough in 1976, when Bubble Yum hit candy stores as the first gum you could blow into a bubble after just a few bites. (Gums before Bubble Yum required a jaw-exhausting break-in period to get them ready to blow.) According to legend, Bubble Yum's chewiness was linked to one icky ingredient: spider eggs (variations of the tale included spider legs and spider webs). Rumors spread that kids who chewed Bubble Yum woke up covered in webs—if they woke up at all!

THE TRUTH: No one knows who spun this particular web of deceit, but Bubble Yum's manufacturer ran full-page advertisements in newspapers across the United States to assure aghast gum chewers that no spiders were farmed in the making of their product.

POP ROCKS AND SODA: A DEADLY COMBO!

THE MYTH: A treat with a mouth-tickling twist, Pop Rocks are pebble-size candies created from a boiling process that combines sugar with carbon-dioxide bubbles. The bubbles burst with a pleasing pop when they touch your tongue, but allegedly those pops grow in explosive power when mixed with the additional carbon dioxide of carbonated soda. According to one popular playground legend, a child actor from a 1980s cereal commercial perished after his stomach exploded from eating packages of Pop Rocks while guzzling soda.

THE TRUTH: Pop Rocks barely pack enough carbon dioxide to trigger a minor burp let alone a stomach-rending explosion, even when combined with a six-pack of pop. And that kid from the cereal commercial? His Pop Rock passing was an invention of pop culture; he's still alive and working in the advertising business in New York City.

Unnatural Disaster

A FLOOD OF DEADLY MUD STAINS EASTERN EUROPE...

WANDER THE HILLS OF WESTERN HUNGARY AND YOU MIGHT SUDDENLY FIND YOURSELF IN AN ALIEN LANDSCAPE. A deep red stain creeps across the fields, forests, and buildings, ending abruptly three feet (1 m) above the ground. It's as if you're standing on the surface of Mars—but only from the legs down.

What could have created such out-of-this-world terrain? In October 2010, the wall of a local industrial-waste reservoir crumbled, spilling more than 180 million gallons (680 million L) of toxic red sludge. The waist-deep flood of mud flowed through nearby villages and eventually oozed over 15 square miles (39 sq km), drowning ten people and burning the skin of more than a hundred others with its chemicals.

Cleanup crews used shovels and hoses to mop up the muck, but the red mud left its mark on everything it touched. Today, the freaky stain serves as a reminder of what can happen when toxic waste runs amok.

MORE SURREAL SPILLS …

STICKY MESS

With a roar of ripping steel and the pop-pop-popping of flying rivets, a towering tank of molasses exploded in Boston in January 1919, unleashing a tidal wave of the sticky syrup onto nearby houses and streets at 34 miles an hour (55 km/h). The disaster claimed the lives of 21 people and injured many more. Some say you can still detect a sweet smell on hot summer days.

FOUL FOAM

Blobs of toxic bubbles bob on the surface of the Tietê River, Brazil's most polluted waterway. The foam forms when water levels drop during the dry season and chemicals from detergent and other runoff become more concentrated.

SWINE FLUME

The German village of Elsa became a sickening swamp in early 2006 after a fertilizer tank burst, flooding the streets with more than 50,000 gallons (190,000 L) of pig poo. No one was hurt, but the knee-deep slop raised quite a stink.

TIM
THE GRIM REAPER'S
FATAL FACTS

These freaky floods scare me to death, but they're not even among the deadliest industrial accidents. As many as 16,000 people died and more than 500,000 were injured when deadly gas leaked from a pesticide plant in India in 1984.

Titanic vs.

ONE SHIP'S FATE WAS SEALED BY A DRIFTING ISLAND OF ICE. THE OTHER VESSEL FOUNDERED IN A BALL OF FIRE. THE FINAL JOURNEYS OF THE *TITANIC* AND THE *HINDENBURG* ENDED IN TWO OF HISTORY'S MOST INFAMOUS FAILURES OF SAFETY SYSTEMS, SHIP DESIGN, AND HUMAN JUDGMENT.

SINKING OF THE *TITANIC*

When it was set to sail on its maiden voyage in 1912, the passenger ship *Titanic* was the largest moving object ever constructed, nearly the length of three football fields and as tall as a 17-story building. It came complete with a heated swimming pool, two barber shops, four elevators, two libraries, and 15 separate watertight compartments that were supposed to keep the ship afloat should any take on water. Its builders insisted it was unsinkable.

History proved them wrong. *Titanic*'s first voyage would be its last. On the night of April 14, 1912, the unsinkable ship struck an iceberg about 400 miles (644 km) southeast of Newfoundland, Canada. The ice slashed a gash in the ship's side under the waterline, flooding five of the watertight compartments. Within three hours, the front of the ship dipped underwater, tipping the stern into the sky until the *Titanic* snapped in half. Both segments sank to the bottom of the North Atlantic, more than two miles (3.2 km) below the icy surface.

Only 32 percent of the ship's 2,223 passengers and crew survived the plunge into the icy ocean. The disaster was all the more tragic because it could have been avoided. The *Titanic* carried only enough lifeboats for about half the people on board, and panic during the sinking led to many lifeboats launching only half full.

No single mistake doomed the *Titanic*. Analysis of the ship's construction showed that the rivets holding it together were weak, causing the hull to shear away at the moment of impact. The watertight compartments were built to withstand a head-on collision rather than a long sideways gash. If the captain—who went down with his ship—had hit the iceberg head-on instead of turning at the last second, *Titanic* might have survived. The ship was also traveling too quickly through iceberg-strewn waters in the days before ice-detecting radar. Ultimately, it was a combination of faulty technology and errors in judgment that sank the "unsinkable" ship.

Hindenburg

CRASH OF THE *HINDENBURG*

Disasters

Decked out with restaurants, libraries, showers, sleeping cabins, and even piano lounges inside their cavernous tube-shaped hulls, airships—also known as zeppelins—carried passengers in the lap of luxury compared to today's cramped passenger planes. Think of zeppelins as cruise ships that soared at 650 feet (200 m). In the early days of air travel, they were the only way to fly for well-to-do passengers with money and time to spare (a typical transatlantic airship trip took nearly five days).

But the technology that kept these vessels in the sky was based on dangerous principles. Invented before airplanes, airships relied on lighter-than-air gas—particularly hydrogen—stored in cells within the ship to stay afloat, while propellers pushed zeppelins through the air at around 75 miles an hour (120 km/h). But hydrogen is highly flammable. Just one fizzy gas leak combined with a spark could turn these flying cruise ships into flaming hulks. Dozens of airships crashed and burned in the early 20th century (today's blimps—the modern equivalents of zeppelins—rely on helium gas, which is more expensive than hydrogen but not flammable).

Germany's fleet of passenger zeppelins had a stellar safety record—more than 2,000 flights over 30 years with no injuries—but that all came crashing down on May 6, 1937. After a mostly smooth flight from its point of origin in Germany, across the Atlantic Ocean, and over New York City, the airship *Hindenburg* descended to 200 feet (60 m) above its destination airfield in Lakehurst, New Jersey, U.S.A. Then, disaster struck! A spark—perhaps caused by a charge in the air after the ship touched the ground with its landing lines—ignited a leak in one of the airship's hydrogen cells. In less than a minute, the largest vessel ever airborne was consumed in a ball of flame. More than half of the airship's 97 passengers and crew members managed to leap to safety. The *Hindenburg*'s fiery demise was captured on newsreel footage later synced to eyewitness reporting by reporter Herbert Morrison. His emotional radio report helped convince the public to travel by plane or train instead. The era of airships was over.

TIM
THE GRIM REAPER'S
FATAL FACTS

The future of air travel is ... a thing of the past? The era of zeppelins might soon resume with the launch of high-tech hotels that drift through the skies like airborne cruise ships (except they'll stay aloft using safer helium gas instead of flammable hydrogen).

BY THIS POINT IN THE BOOK, YOU MIGHT THINK ALL TECHNOLOGY IS OUT TO KILL YOU. **NOT TRUE!** REASSURE YOURSELF WITH THIS TOUR OF NEAR-FUTURE GEAR THAT COULD BE SAVING LIVES BY 2020 ...

That's NOT Deadly!

New tech set might one day save lives rather than take them ...

ROADS WILL BE SAFER ONCE DRIVERS TAKE THEIR HANDS OFF THE WHEEL. In the next few years, we could hop into self-driving cars that use lasers to "see" the road and sensors to keep a safe distance between other cars. Your robo-chauffeur does the driving while you sit in the back and play video games.

MACHINES THAT PRINT REAL-LIFE OBJECTS—from chess pieces to combs to rubber duckies—already exist, but soon doctors will use these 3-D printers to create replacement organs. A new ticker or kidney could be just a button press away!

IF IT'S A DIRTY JOB, NOBODY WILL HAVE TO DO IT. Robot workers will replace humans when it comes to dangerous work. NASA is already developing humanoid space robots that technicians will control from Earth.

TIM
THE GRIM REAPER'S
FATAL FACTS

Before the invention of modern medical sensors, accidental burial was a very real danger! Doctors relied on all kinds of horrible methods to make sure people had actually expired before they could be buried, including poking the bodies with hot rods and connecting bells from their coffins to their tombstones using ropes.

MICROSCOPIC MEDICAL "NANOBOTS" WILL SWARM THROUGH YOUR BLOODSTREAM like miniature mechanical bees to replace your body's old cells and cure diseases, increasing your life span by hundreds of years.

ROBOT SURGEONS WILL PERFORM ROUTINE OPERATIONS or allow your doctor to examine you from across the country.

LISTEN TO YOUR JACKET— it will try to save your life! Computers and sensors sewn into the fabric will warn of incoming traffic if you forget to look both ways.

PIG OUT ON ALL THE CANDY BARS AND FATTY BURGERS YOU WANT IN 30 YEARS—as long as you follow it up with a "nutribot" pill. Microscopic robots inside the pill zap all the junk in your junk food.

ANCIENT DESTRUCTION EQUIPMENT

TREBUCHET

As many as 60 men worked this giant medieval slingshot, which relied on a massive counterweight to hurl boulders the distance of three football fields (much farther than standard catapults, called mangonels). Trebuchet crews could smash castle walls and the defenders behind them while remaining safely out of arrowshot. Trebuchets could also hurl flaming casks and even the bodies of plague victims to spread disease within the castle—an early example of biological warfare!

BALLISTA

When armies needed to halt charging enemies or take fortresses in ancient Greece and Rome, they broke out machinery designed to damage more than stone walls. Case in point: the ballista. This supersize crossbow launched giant arrows up to 500 yards (460 m), skewering defenders. They could also be loaded with stone ammunition for castle-crashing sieges.

BATTERING RAM

An ancient weapon, the battering ram was built to bash big holes in castle walls and gates (in battles called sieges). It consisted of a heavy wooden post—often topped with the sculpture of a ram's head—hung from ropes beneath a roofed structure on wheels. The besiegers could roll the ram right up to enemy gates while the defenders above mounted a furious defense, raining arrows and boiling water on their attackers. The castle garrison would try to drop straw mattresses in front of the ram to absorb its impact.

GATE Crashers

KILL-O-METER

DANGEROUS DEVICES

TIM
THE GRIM REAPER
RANKS MAJOR MALFUNCTIONS

Kill-O-Meter	
SUDDEN DEATH	Nest of Bees
RUN FOR YOUR LIFE!	Boston Molasses Flood
DANGER ZONE	Ford Pinto
RISKY BUSINESS	Exploding Cell Phones
	Lawn Darts

CHAPTER 6

Toxic Shockers

WARNING: THE FOLLOWING CHAPTER CONTAINS TOPICS THAT ARE TERRIBLE TO THE TOUCH AND DEADLY IF SWALLOWED.

Symptoms within include severe sweating, squirming in your seat, and feelings of ickiness, followed by a general sense of dread. You'll encounter titanic insects with lethal stings, slithering serpents with venomous bites, and jellyfish with enough stinging power to send you sprinting for shore. A witch's brew of bad medicine lies ahead, so heed the skull-and-crossbones warning and proceed with extreme caution.

VENOMOUS OR

What's the difference?

YOU MIGHT THINK "POISON" AND "VENOM" ARE INTERCHANGEABLE TERMS FOR THE SAME TERRIBLE THING. NOPE! ALTHOUGH BOTH ARE TOXINS, OR DANGEROUS SUBSTANCES THAT CAN RUIN YOUR DAY (AND PERHAPS END

Venomous Offenders

Venomous creatures—including snakes, spiders, lizards, and even some snails—take the direct approach, squirting toxin directly into the bloodstream of their victims using a body part (such as fangs, stingers, or spines) adapted specifically for venom injection. The toxin is almost always produced in the animal's body, typically in a gland near the injector. Many venomous creatures evolved their chemical weapons for offense: to kill or stun prey for an easier meal. These animals can also control the dose of venom they inject for defensive reasons. More than 20 percent of all bites from venomous snakes, for instance, are "dry bites," inflicted without venom to send a clear warning: "Back off, or the next bite will pack a nasty surprise!"

Venomous Specimen
ASIAN GIANT HORNET

"Big" and "bad" barely begin to describe the Asian giant hornet, a bulbous bug with a body the size of your thumb and wings that span your hand. Its quarter-inch (6-cm) stinger injects venom that dissolves flesh and feels like a hot nail. Honeybees have the most to fear from these oversize insects. Just a few Asian giant hornets can tear through 10,000 bees, leaving behind nothing but bit-off heads and legs. About 40 people die each year from allergic reactions to the hornet's sting.

ICKY INGREDIENTS

Venoms and poisons combine special proteins called enzymes and other chemicals into bad brews divided into these two broad types ...

NEUROTOXINS make the victim shake uncontrollably or go numb from head to toe, leading to paralysis and death.

HEMOTOXINS destroy skin and internal organs and can block the body's ability to stop the flow of blood. Left untreated, victims can bleed to death.

POiSONOUS?

YOUR LIFE), POISONS AND VENOMS ARE DIFFERENT IN ONE KEY ASPECT: THE WAY THEY ENTER THE VICTIM'S BODY. BEFORE WE DIVE TOO DEEPLY INTO THIS CHAPTER'S TOXIC TOPICS, LET'S TAKE A MINUTE TO MAKE CLEAR THIS DISTINCTION IN WILDLIFE CHEMICAL WARFARE ...

Poisonous Defenders

Poisonous animals—which include many frogs, butterflies, beetles, grasshoppers, and even some mammals—don't inject their toxins using fangs or stingers like venomous creatures do. Instead, they contain poison within their bodies or as secretions on their skin. Victims are exposed to the toxin only if they nibble on (or sometimes even touch) the poisonous animal, making the poison a purely defensive adaptation. Poisonous creatures often absorb the toxins through their diet rather than create them inside their bodies. They're also brightly colored to warn predators to steer clear. Hungry animals that take a taste risk more than an upset stomach; their first bite could be their last.

Poisonous Specimen
POISON DART FROG

Red, green, blue, yellow, gold, copper—name a color and you'll spot it on the vivid skin of this rain forest resident, which varies in hue depending on where it lives from Costa Rica to Brazil. Poison dart frogs bear their vibrant hues for a reason: to warn predators to look but not lick. Their skin secretes one of the most toxic substances on Earth. The toxin of the two-inch (5-cm) golden poison dart frog is lethal enough to kill ten grown humans. For centuries, Colombia's Emberá people have dipped their blowgun darts in the poison before hunting.

TIM
THE GRIM REAPER'S
FATAL FACTS

Can you believe poisons and venoms are being used to save lives? Chemists have mined these chemicals to concoct drugs that relieve high-blood pressure, target cancer cells, relieve arthritis, and treat diseases. Hey, that's bad for my business!

119

STRIKING DISTANCE

Face-to-fang with a deadly snake...

COILED LIKE A SPRING, MOUTH WIDE, FANGS AT THE READY, an angry cottonmouth snake is one of nature's perfect weapons, poised to strike in the blink of an eye. Found slithering and swimming through the swamps of the southeastern United States, this serpent isn't the deadliest of the roughly 375 venomous snakes in the world, but it's still more than capable of killing. Here's how the cottonmouth—and other venomous serpents—deliver sudden death ...

FOUL FACTORIES

Snake venom is produced by special glands in the creature's head, located where the upper and lower jaws join. These venom factories are similar to your saliva glands, except they make toxins instead of mouth-moistening spit. Different snakes produce different kinds of venom. Deadly coral snakes produce neurotoxins that wreck the nervous system, while cottonmouths inject hemotoxins that interfere with the blood clotting. Untreated victims can die by bleeding from every hole in their bodies!

TROUBLE SHOOTERS

As if snakes with needles for teeth aren't scary enough, some species of cobras can spit their venom more than eight feet (2.5 m). These spitting snakes have extra holes in their fangs that let them eject venom as well as inject it. They can spray with terrifying accuracy and often aim for the eyes (their venom can cause temporary blindness). Spitting cobras spit to defend themselves rather than to attack prey.

HEAT SEEKERS

A cottonmouth is a special kind of snake called a pit viper, a group that includes rattlesnakes and copperheads. They didn't earn the name because they live in pits; instead, these serpents possess special heat-sensing organs in pits between their nostrils and eyes. The organs detect even the slightest rise in temperature against the background, giving the snakes a sixth sense for hunting at night.

TOXIC TEETH

You think getting a shot at the doctor is scary? The fangs of many venomous snakes work just like the hypodermic needles your doctor uses to give you shots. When a cottonmouth strikes, muscles near its venom glands squeeze the toxic spit through a small tube in its fangs, injecting venom directly into the wound and the victim's bloodstream. Cottonmouths belong to a group of snakes with fangs that fold against the roofs of their mouths when they're not needed. Some snakes have fixed fangs like a vampire's, while others have teeth that are grooved like a slide instead of hollow like a hypodermic needle. The venom rides the slide into the snake's victim.

SERIOUSLY SCARY SNAKES

THE WORLD'S MOST VENOMOUS SERPENTS, LISTED IN ORDER OF LETHALITY ...

Black Mamba

WHERE IT LIVES: plains and rocky hills of Africa

Named for the dark color of its mouth, which it flashes when in attack mode, this legendary African serpent is terrifying for two reasons: It can slither faster than most people can run, and its venom can kill in just 20 minutes if the victim doesn't receive treatment with antivenom. Fortunately, the black mamba relies on its extreme speed to escape threats rather than attack.

ONCE BITTEN: Black mamba venom attacks the nervous system and can cause the heart to stop.

LEAST LETHAL

Belcher's Sea Snake

WHERE IT LIVES: waters off Australia and in the Indian Ocean

Some of the world's most venomous snakes live in the ocean. The Belcher's sea snake swims through the waters off northern Australia and Southeast Asia. But although its venom is among the world's deadliest, this shy and docile serpent rarely bites humans.

ONCE BITTEN: Sea snake venom contains neurotoxins that slowly immobilize the victims until they stop breathing.

Tiger Snake

WHERE IT LIVES: Australia and Tasmania

These serpents of southern Australia come with a double dose of danger. They inject deadly venom from their fangs and secrete poison from their skin. That makes them one of the few animals that are both poisonous and venomous. In other words, tiger snakes can kill whether they bite or are bitten.

ONCE BITTEN: Tiger snake bites cause immediate weakness, bleeding, and kidney failure.

Russel's Viper

WHERE IT LIVES: India and Southeast Asia

The deadliest of the "big four," the quartet of serpents responsible for the most snake deaths in India, this pit viper lurks in houses, barns, and fields hunting for rodents. Unfortunately, humans sometimes get in the way.

ONCE BITTEN: The viper's venom is a foul cocktail of toxins that can cause organs to shut down.

MOST LETHAL

Taipan

WHERE IT LIVES: inland Australia

This speedy serpent has the most toxic venom of any land snake. A drop smaller than the period at the end of this sentence could wipe out a thousand mice. One bite packs enough venom to kill more than a hundred humans, which is why you always want to shake out your sleeping bag before crawling in for the night while camping in Australia.

ONCE BITTEN: Taipan venom is a deadly neurotoxin that remains lethal even after 80 years in storage.

TIM
THE GRIM REAPER'S
FATAL FACTS

Newborn rattlesnakes are the world's deadliest babies, born with venom already in their glands. They're even more dangerous than adult rattle-snakes because they haven't learned how to withhold venom when delivering warning bites.

SNAKE CHARMER

SURVIVING ONE VENOMOUS SNAKEBITE IS HARROWING ENOUGH. TIM THE GRIM REAPER INTERVIEWS A "MILK MAN" WHO'S BEEN BITTEN EIGHT TIMES AND LIVED TO TALK ABOUT IT ...

WHEN JIM HARRISON HAS A BAD DAY AT THE OFFICE, HE MIGHT END IT WITH A TRIP TO THE HOSPITAL. As the director of the Kentucky Reptile Zoo, home to the largest collection of venomous snakes in the world, Harrison works in a nest of vipers (and cobras, and many other deadly serpents). He "milks" as many as a thousand deadly snakes each day by pressing their fangs against a beaker and collecting their venom. The toxin is then used for research into lifesaving medicines and antivenom serums to treat snakebite victims. It's a dangerous job—and Harrison has the scars to prove it—but somebody has to do it. Meet the man whose job really bites ...

TIM: How long have you been excited about snakes?
HARRISON: About 50 years. Since I was six years old!

TIM: Why did snakes sink their teeth into you? Well, figuratively speaking...
HARRISON: I caught a snake at a family reunion—just a harmless garter snake. I had no frame of reference and thought the snake was really neat. But when I showed it to adults, many of them freaked out. I was fascinated by this small, beautiful animal that I did not see as threatening at all, yet it was able to terrify many adults.

TIM: Does milking more than a hundred snakes a day get boring?
HARRISON: It does become routine, and we have to guard against complacency. I try to look at it as a marathon and keep plugging away. If you get bored when working with them, that is when one will surprise you!

TIM: Of the eight times you've been bitten, which was the worst?
HARRISON: The worst bite was from a lancehead viper, a type of snake from Brazil. It is hard to know if I would have died from the bite; we certainly were not going to delay treatment to see how bad it was! This bite was the worst because it had a lot of complications and my wrist has permanent damage from it.

TIM: Yikes! I bet that hurt.
HARRISON: It hurt so much that the breeze from a fan was painful.

TIM: What'd you do wrong that you were bit?
HARRISON: I underestimated the ability of the snake. I thought my hand was out of its reach, but I was wrong.

TIM: What's the first thing that springs to mind when you're bitten on the job?
HARRISON: We do have a protocol that is followed in the event of a bite. I do not panic or freak out, I just do what needs to be done to take care of it. Later I might get upset because I made a mistake, but at the time the focus is simply on taking care of it.

TIM: Is there any species of snake you're afraid to mess with?
HARRISON: No.

TIM: What would you say to people who get creeped out around snakes?
HARRISON: Even though some snakes can hurt you, no snake wants to. Snakes are very shy and easily frightened; they are just small animals trying to survive. All snakes will run away if they can. Most bites occur to people who are intentionally coming into contact with them—trying to catch or kill them. People who leave snakes alone are rarely bitten. Also, [medications] were developed from snake venom, so snakes have saved more lives than they have ever taken.

125

OPPOSITES ATTACK
MONGOOSE

Somewhere on the sandy plains of southern India, a mongoose has scurried into the path of a slithering cobra. Uh-oh! Surely the mongoose is a goner, right? Not quite. Meet these ancient enemies and see a breakdown of their battle. Spoiler alert: The winner might surprise you ...

INDIAN GRAY MONGOOSE

Think of mongooses as the Clark Kents (Superman's alter ego) of the animal world, mild-mannered and curious as they scour their territory for mice, lizards, birds, worms, and eggs. But when this cat-size mammal encounters a cobra or other venomous threat, it transforms into a bold little beast with Superman-like powers of speed and invincibility.

The Indian gray mongoose of southern India thrives in the dusty farmland and grassy plains near houses and other dwellings. Here, humans welcome their presence. Not only do mongooses control mice and other pests, but they're fearless in the face of venomous snakes. Cobras are just another treat on the mongoose's menu! The mammal's snake-beating feats inspired the fictional Rikki-tikki-tavi, a fearsome mongoose who wages a war against cobras in author Rudyard Kipling's *The Jungle Book*.

HISS AND MISS

Equipped with lightning reflexes, mongooses have an instinctive ability to battle venomous snakes. They remain calm in the face of a cobra's terrifying strike, watching and waiting for their chance to counterattack. Mongooses also have a thick coat of fur that deflects snakebites. Research has shown that these feisty animals have one final secret weapon: a slight immunity to the cobra's venom. They can shake off a strike and keep fighting.

TIM THE GRIM REAPER'S FATAL FACTS

The mongoose isn't just bad news for cobras. It's a dangerous invasive species in Puerto Rico and Hawaii, where it was introduced in the 1800s to eat pests on sugar plantations. With no natural predators, the hungry little mammals now threaten many bird species native to the islands.

VS. COBRA

INDIAN COBRA

In one movement, almost too fast to see, the Indian cobra rears up on its tail and fans out its hood, a disc of scaly skin that makes the snake look scarier. *Hisss!* You don't need to know Parseltongue—serpent-speak in the wizarding world of Harry Potter—to get this snake's message: "Back off!" The cobra is poised to strike.

Indian cobras are one of the "big four" serpents responsible for the most human snakebite deaths in India. Shy snakes that hide during the day, they prey on mice, frogs, and lizards. Unfortunately, humans occasionally stumble across these serpents, which become aggressive when startled. When that happens, an Indian cobra rises up to a third of its body length, nearly three feet (1 m) off the ground. By extending the ribs of its neck, the cobra can flare out its iconic hood, which makes the snake appear larger and more intimidating. An aggressive cobra will sway back and forth, as if to hypnotize its prey, while unleashing a deep hiss that sounds like an angry dog.

The Indian cobra's venom, which it injects through hollow fangs, is a brew of toxins that can paralyze muscles and cause heart attacks in victims unless they receive treatment with antivenom (which is widely available). These snakes don't strike like rattlesnakes or other coiling serpents. Instead, they rear up and fall on their victims with enough force to drive their fangs into flesh.

TOXIC TEETH

WHICH IS MORE DEADLY? THE MONGOOSE!

Cobras are fast, but mongooses are faster. When its enemy lunges to bite, the mongoose dances just out of reach before pouncing on the cobra's head and crushing its skull in powerful jaws. Score one for the mammals!

CREEPING

THE WORLD'S DEADLIEST INSECTS AND ARACHNIDS

BLACK WIDOW SPIDER
WHERE IT LIVES: NORTH AMERICA

These itsy-bitsy biters are easy to identify by the red hourglass shape on their black bodies. They're the most venomous spiders in North America (their venom is said to be 15 times more powerful than a rattlesnake's). Although rarely fatal, the black widow's bite can cause nausea, achy muscles, and difficulty breathing. This skittish spider relies on its venom to hunt insects rather than kill people. Females sometimes slay and devour their mates, hence the species' sinister name.

AFRICANIZED BEE
WHERE IT LIVES: FROM SOUTH AMERICA TO THE SOUTHEASTERN UNITED STATES

The product of an experiment gone wrong, this highly aggressive breed of honeybee escaped from a lab in Brazil in 1957 and has been heading north ever since. They'll pursue any threat until it drops—and then keep on stinging and stinging and stinging! A swarm chasing a Texas man pierced him with more than a thousand stings! Known to scientists as Africanized bees, they were dubbed "killer bees" by the media.

WORLD OF HURT
The bite of the conga ant, which scurries through the rain forests of Central and South America, won't kill you, but you might wish it at least knocked you out. It's been ranked as the most painful insect bite in the world! The ant's venom causes a throbbing, fiery pain that victims compare to being shot, hence this insect's alternate name: the bullet ant.

KILLERS

DEATHSTALKER SCORPION
WHERE IT LIVES: THE DESERTS OF NORTH AFRICA AND THE MIDDLE EAST

Scorpions inject more than just fear when they're spotted scurrying across the floor. Their tails are tipped with a stinger that works like a needle to squirt venom into victims. Scorpion stings are painful (people who have been stung compare the sensation to getting jabbed by a hot nail), but most species aren't deadly. The deathstalker is one scary exception. Its venom contains neurotoxins that can kill infants and the elderly, although healthy kids and adults usually survive the agonizing sting.

TIM
THE GRIM REAPER'S
FATAL FACTS

Can you believe the deathstalker scorpion is a popular pet? Hey, that makes my job easier ...

SYDNEY FUNNEL-WEB SPIDER
WHERE IT LIVES: IN AND AROUND SYDNEY, AUSTRALIA

A large spider with a lousy attitude, this Australia native rears up on hairy legs and brandishes its venomous fangs to anyone who provokes it. Once in attack mode, the spider will bite and bite and bite some more. Victims could croak in an hour if they don't receive the widely available antivenom. Because of its powerful neurotoxin, aggressive attitude, and proximity to people, the Sydney funnel-web is considered the world's deadliest spider.

MOSQUITO
WHERE IT LIVES: AFRICA AND TROPICAL AND MILD CLIMATES AROUND THE WORLD

It's not really accurate to lump this buzzing, bothersome fly in with other venomous bugs, but the mosquito's bite spreads something much more dangerous than venom: disease. Millions of people perish each year from mosquito bites in Africa and elsewhere. The bloodsucking flies spread malaria, dengue fever, and other illnesses that are fatal if left untreated.

STINGING SENSATION

The box jellyfish is all pain and no brains …

ONE OF THE DEADLIEST CREATURES ON EARTH IS A BONELESS, BRAINLESS BLOB THAT BOBS IN THE WARM COASTAL WATERS OF NORTHERN AUSTRALIA. Called the box jellyfish, it's not as nightmarish in appearance as a killer bee or a deathstalker scorpion, but those killer creepers wield only one stinger apiece. The box jellyfish carries tens of thousands. Each is loaded with venom that can kill a human in less than five minutes.

ALSO STRANGELY VENOMOUS …

Among jellyfish, the box jellyfish is at the head of its class. It's able to swim, for instance, rather than just drift with the currents. It also has sophisticated eyes—24 of them, grouped in clusters of 6 on all four sides of its box-shaped body (hence its name). Dangling from its corners are as many as 15 tentacles that can reach ten feet (3 m) in length, and each tentacle bristles with more than 5,000 stinging cells.

Jellyfish stingers—called nematocysts—are like tiny hollow harpoons. They launch by the thousands when the jellyfish's tentacle detects certain chemicals on the surface of its prey (typically fish or shrimp, although human skin will trigger them, too). The harpoons lodge in the skin and inject toxins that damage flesh, shut down the nervous system, and can even stop the heart. It's estimated that one box jellyfish carries enough venom to kill 60 humans. The jellyfish evolved with such powerful venom for a reason: It kills fish instantly so they don't damage the jellyfish's delicate tentacles in their death throes.

Box jellyfish don't seek out human victims. Most encounters result from bad luck, when humans accidentally brush against the creature's tentacles in murky water. The stings are so excruciating that some victims have drowned because of shock or heart attack. Survivors describe an agony that lasts for weeks. They carry the scars—long streaks on the skin wherever the tentacles made contact—for the rest of their lives.

KOMODO DRAGON

Researchers used to think these titanic Indonesian lizards—which grow up to ten feet (3 m) long—were deadly solely for the infectious saliva in their germ-ridden mouths. But it turns out komodo dragons have venomous fangs just like snakes. A dragon will rip open prey with its razorlike teeth, then patiently follow the stricken animal until it dies of blood loss or poisoning. Once its yucky mouth has done its dirty work, the lizard moves in for the feast.

CONE SNAILS

Slow and deadly, this six-inch (15-cm) snail creeps along the seafloor of the Indo-Pacific at night, sniffing out snoozing fish. Once it finds its victim, the cone snail engulfs it with a tubelike mouth and flushes a sort of sleeping potion over the fish's gills. Trapped in its worst nightmare, the paralyzed fish sits helpless until the cone snail jabs it with a harpoonlike tooth that injects a deadly toxin—which occasionally kills humans.

PLATYPUS

With the bill and feet of a duck, the furry body of an otter, and the tail of a beaver, the Australian platypus seems like an animal thrown together from spare parts. And if its appearance isn't weird enough, this aquatic mammal is also venomous! Males wield a stinger on the r webbed feet that injects a toxin powerful enough to kill small animals.

PICKING THEIR POISONS

TWO FAMOUS FIGURES CHOOSE THEIR BITTER ENDS ...

SOCRATES

DATE OF DEATH: **399 B.C.**

A Greek philosopher and teacher famous for developing the Socratic method (or learning by asking questions), Socrates was put on trial by a small group of wealthy nobles in Athens. They accused him of corrupting the youth and mocking the Greek gods. Socrates thought the trial was ridiculous and barely bothered defending himself. He offered to pay a small fine, but the jury sentenced him to death instead. Given several excruciating options for his execution, Socrates chose poison. He drank it himself, then walked among his students until his legs gave out.

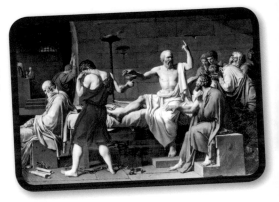

POISON OF CHOICE: **HEMLOCK**
The sap of this deadly plant, supposedly favored by witches for killing potions, causes seizures and death when eaten or even touched.

ANCIENT TOXIN TESTERS

SHARKS' TEETH: Europeans dipped fossilized sharks' teeth—which they believed were dragon tongues—into food to cleanse it of any poisons.

JADE CUPS: Europeans thought vessels made of jade would detoxify wine.

HORNBILL UTENSILS: Malaysians believed that spoons made from the beaks of hornbill birds would change color if they touched a poisonous substance.

TIM
THE GRIM REAPER'S
FATAL FACTS

Peasants across 17th-century Europe feared wolf's bane for its supposed ability to transform people into fearsome werewolves.

CLEOPATRA VII
DATE OF DEATH: 30 B.C.

This brilliant and bewitching Greek queen became one of ancient Egypt's most famous pharaohs—as well as its last. She was the first in her line of foreign rulers to learn the Egyptian language, and she expanded the temples of knowledge in the Egyptian city of Alexandria. She used her cunning to win support from rival Rome while also struggling to maintain Egypt's independence. She had love affairs with the Roman generals Julius Caesar and Mark Antony. After Antony committed suicide because of a lost battle, Cleopatra followed suit by cuddling up with an Egyptian cobra. Or so went the legend. Some historians believe Cleopatra, an expert on poisons, wouldn't have relied on a painful and unreliable snakebite to end her life. Instead, she likely mixed her own toxic brew to ensure a fast and relatively painless passing.

POISON OF CHOICE: WOLF'S BANE

This toxic flower was plucked from mountain meadows and used in many painless poison potions. It also goes by the name Dumbledore's Delight. ("Dumbledore" is an old word for bumblebee.)

DEATH FISH

FATAL **FUGU** IS A MEAL FOR THRILL SEEKERS ...

EVERY WINTER, IN SOME OF JAPAN'S FINEST RESTAURANTS, CUSTOMERS PAY UP TO $200 FOR A MEAL THAT MIGHT BE THEIR LAST. They order fugu, or blowfish, a spiny kind of fish packed with a poison said to be 1,200 times more lethal than deadly cyanide. When prepared correctly, fugu (pronounced foo-goo) contains just enough toxin to make the diner's tongue tingle. When prepared incorrectly, that tingle grows to a numbness of the mouth, then paralysis and death by suffocation. The victim stays conscious through the entire ordeal. There is no antidote.

Fugu is such a deadly dish that its preparation has been outlawed several times in Japan's history. Today, Japan's elite fugu chefs must undergo years of special training and earn a license from the government to serve the dish. Preparing the fish is a little like defusing a bomb. Wielding razor-sharp knives, a fugu chef carefully removes the fish's ovaries, liver, and intestines. These are the poisonous parts, filled with tetrodotoxins that attack the victim's nervous system. A single blowfish contains enough tetrodotoxin to kill 30 people. Chefs then check and recheck that they removed all the poison before preparing the fillet. The offending organs are dumped into a metal container and burned.

More than 20 people have died in Japan from eating fugu since the year 2000 (victims are usually fishermen who prepared their deadly catch themselves). Thousands of restaurants serve up to 10,000 tons of fugu—often raw as sashimi—each year. It's both a delicacy and a popular dish among thrill seekers. Fugu aficionados say it has a rich, chewy texture but barely any taste. Which begs the question: Would you risk your life for a bite of a flavorless fish?

CYANIDE ON THE SIDE
MORE DEADLY DELICACIES ...

MUSHROOMS

Relax—the mushrooms on your pizza are safe for consumption. But these funky fungi come in so many deadly and mind-altering varieties (bad mushrooms are called toadstools) that you should never pick your own from the forest floor. After all, you wouldn't want to mix up the appropriately named death cap with a garden-variety 'shroom just for the sake of a fresh salad.

CASU MARZU

In the Sardinian region of Italy, food lovers treasure this black-market cheese, which is deliberately left outdoors for flies to fill with their eggs. The result is a cheesy mass of maggot poop that can cause severe intestinal illness. Connoisseurs of this rancid rind eat it with safety glasses—protection against leaping maggots.

BULLFROGS

A big frog with a bigger problem, these football-size amphibians are such a popular dish in the African country of Namibia that their numbers are threatened. But bullfrogs are also bad news for the people who eat them during frog mating season, when they can contain a powerful poison that causes kidney failure if consumed.

TIM
THE GRIM REAPER'S
FATAL FACTS

Fugu chefs face the ultimate test during their training. For the final exam, they must eat their own fugu dish!

KOALAS

Koalas don't live in eucalyptus trees just because they enjoy the view. These icons of the Australian bush clamber up the branches to munch on the trees one leaf at a time, eating up to a pound (0.45 kg) per day. The leaves are tough to digest, provide little nutrition, and—worst of all—are poisonous! Koalas have a specially adapted digestive system that ekes every drop of energy from the leaves while neutralizing their toxins.

POISON
CONTROL

MEERKATS

These feisty members of the mongoose family don't turn tail and skedaddle when they spot a scorpion on the dusty plains of southern Africa. Instead, they ring the school bell! Meerkats learn from an early age how to beat and eat scorpions, their favorite snack. Adult meerkats will tear off a scorpion's tail, then bring the wriggling arachnid back to the burrow for hunting practice with the younger members of the group (called a mob). The students grow up to become expert scorpion exterminators.

HONEY BADGERS

Built like bodybuilding skunks, these ferocious African mammals have a reputation for scrappiness and a seeming invincibility to toxins that would terminate larger creatures. They won't let a few hundred stings stop them from bulldozing headfirst into a honeybee hive and devouring the yummy larvae. Bites from puff adders, cobras, and other deadly snakes barely slow the honey badger's stride, thanks to its thick skin and slight immunity to the venom.

TOXIN-
Blocking
ANIMALS

SUDDEN DEATH

RUN FOR YOUR LIFE!

DANGER ZONE

RISKY BUSINESS

Box Jellyfish

Taipan

Funnel-web Spider

Tiger Snake

Platypus

KILL-O-METER

BITTER **BITES**

TIM
THE GRIM REAPER
RANKS TOXIC MONSTERS

CHAPTER 7

Danger Zones

LAVA-SPEWING VOLCANOES, SKY-SCRAPER LEDGES, BEACHES BATTERED BY COLOSSAL WAVES—these scary places don't need "DANGER" signs to warn people away. But sometimes serene scenery can disguise a deadly destination, hiding hazards until it's too late. Watch your step during this tour of the world's scenic dangers, fatal attractions, and deadliest spots—some of which are closer than your own backyard!

KILLER CONTINENT:
AUSTRALIA

Australia is famous for its cute koalas, hopping kangaroos, and heart-stopping vistas, but this rugged wonderland is also home to the world's deadliest animals and terrain that could actually stop your heart. Here's why the land down under is a wonderful place to visit, but you wouldn't want to die there ...

STINGER SEASON

Take a dip off Australia's northern beaches from October to May and you risk swimming into a swarm of "sea wasps," aka box jellyfish. The world's deadliest jellyfish (see page 130), they inject an agonizing venom that can stop the heart and kill in minutes. Beaches post warnings when these seasonal schools are sighted off the coast.

OUTBACK ATTACK

Beginning where civilization ends, the "outback" is a catchall term for Australia's sunburnt heart, a region larger than Texas, U.S.A. Fewer than 60,000 people live in this wasteland of deserts, rocky hills, and sparse scrubland, making it popular with outdoor enthusiasts who want to get far, far, far away from it all. Get lost here, however, and you risk dying from sun exposure or thirst—if a venomous snake or spider doesn't get you first!

SPIDER CENTRAL

You already had the displeasure of meeting the Sydney funnel-web spider on page 129, but it's hardly the only awful arachnid in Australia. Redback spiders live in proximity to people and deliver a bite as bad as a black widow's (see page 128). Australia is also home to the bird-eating tarantula, which grows to the size of a baseball catcher's mitt and feeds on hatchlings, rodents, and insects that wander into its burrow.

SHARK CENTRAL

The world's three deadliest shark species—great whites, bull sharks, and tiger sharks (see page 37)—inhabit the waters around Australia, and more than 190 people have died in shark attacks here since 1788. Surfers and spearfishers have the most to fear, although pedestrians might want to watch out. Residents near Brisbane, Queensland, reported seeing bull sharks swimming in their streets during a 2011 flood!

DEAD RINGER

Ancient mariners feared the kraken, a titanic tentacled sea monster said to wreck ships. Turns out it wasn't the big eight-legged monster they had to worry about. Australia's Great Barrier Reef is home to the blue-ringed octopus, a golfball-size creature with three hearts, blue blood, and enough venom to kill 26 people with one bite. A shy and stunning creature, it pulses blue rings on its color-shifting skin when threatened. Smart divers know to keep their distance. The octopus's lethal venom—the same chemical carried in blowfish (see page 134)—has no antidote.

TOOTHY TERROR

More than 4,400 pounds (2,000 kg) of teeth, armored skin, and aggressive attitude, saltwater crocodiles (see page 49) lurk in the rivers, swamps, and lakes along the coasts of northern Australia. But they're easy to avoid if you follow one simple rule: Stay out of the water.

FEARSOME FLOCK

Armed with daggerlike claws up to 5 inches (13 cm) long and a bony spear point atop its head, the southern cassowary of Australia's rain forests certainly looks the part of the "world's most dangerous bird." The reality doesn't live up to the legend (cassowaries are responsible for just one confirmed human fatality in the past century), but you still wouldn't want to get within striking distance of this flightless bird's flesh-rending talons.

TERRIBLE TREE

Even Australia's trees can be dangerous. Leaves of the Australian nettle tree, found in Queensland, have tiny hairs that attach to your skin and cause a stinging pain that can last for months. The stings aren't fatal, but the treatment—which involves hot wax to remove the hairs—is as painful as the symptoms!

STRIKE ZONE

Australia is the only place in the world where the venomous snakes—including sea snakes, the inland taipan, and the tiger snake—outnumber the nonvenomous ones (read about them on page 122). Fortunately, most of these serpents live far from civilization.

TIM
THE GRIM REAPER'S
FATAL FACTS

Scientists suspect that Australia's brutal outback is to blame for the continent's many dangerous creatures. Because water and food are hard to come by here, outback creatures evolved with venomous stings and bites to help them compete for the scarce resources.

EUROPE'S FOGGY WETLANDS OFFER **GRUESOME GLIMPSES** INTO THE PAST ...

BOG BODIES

This ancient Irish king died in style. His hair was pressed into a neat pile above his brow—forming a pompadour that would turn heads today—using a gel made of oil and tree sap imported from France. The last thing he likely saw, in the split second before his death, was the blur of an axe blade arcing toward his head. The king's body tumbled into the murky water of the Irish peat bog, where it lay undisturbed for more than 2,000 years. When his remarkably well-preserved corpse was pulled from the bog in 2003 by a peat-cutting machine, the king's hair—dyed orange by chemicals in the water—was still impeccably styled.

Named the Clonycavan Man for the town in Ireland near his discovery, the king is just one of hundreds of "bog bodies" uncovered in the foggy peat bogs of Ireland, Germany, the Netherlands, and Denmark. Plant matter and a lack of oxygen in the bogs tans and preserves the bodies to an astonishing degree; they still have fingerprints and beard stubble! People who discovered bog bodies actually called the police, thinking these all-natural mummies were recent murder victims.

Northwest Europe's bogs—chilly, remote wetlands mined for iron ore and peat grass that can be burned as fuel—may seem like strange final resting places for the bodies of kings and commoners, children and elderly people, the sick and the healthy (bog bodies come from all walks of ancient life). But people 2,000 years ago believed these bogs were magical portals to another world inhabited by gods and restless spirits. Archaeologists suspect many bodies discovered in the bogs were sacrificed to please these gods. High-ranking people—such as the Clonycavan Man—made the best sacrifices.

Because they are so well preserved, bodies pulled from the bogs provide a glimpse into life during the Iron Age. Scientists are certain more bodies lie hidden in the bogs, waiting to be pulled from these portals to another world.

FAMOUS BOG BODIES

Scientists suspect that Red Franz, named for hair dyed by acids in a German bog, was a horseman murdered nearly 2,000 years ago.

Discovered near the Clonycavan Man, Oldcroghan Man had manicured fingernails to die for! He was also likely a high-ranking sacrifice.

Discovered in a Danish bog in 1950, Tollund Man still bore the rope around his neck used to sacrifice him to the gods 2,300 years ago.

TIM
THE GRIM REAPER'S
FATAL FACTS

The prospect of bumping into a bog body doesn't deter contestants from diving into the murky waters of Wales's Waen Rhydd peat bog every August to compete in the annual World Bog Snorkeling Championships.

OH, Wow!

Four natural wonders that might kill you ...

ANTELOPE CANYON
(ARIZONA, U.S.A.)

Oh, wow!
Vivid bands of red and orange streak along a snaking hallway of sheer sandstone walls—in some places so narrow you can touch both sides—in this frequently photographed canyon, which looks like a geological watercolor painting.

Oh, no!
Like all "slot canyons," Antelope Canyon was carved out of sandstone by raging torrents of rainwater over millions of years, and the process continues today. The canyon can flood in minutes during the rainy monsoon season, even from distant storms. Eleven tourists perished in 1997 when a flash flood sent a wall of water 30 feet (9.1 m) high charging through the canyon.

LAKE NYOS
(CAMEROON, AFRICA)

Oh, wow!
A calm body of deep-blue water surrounded by rolling green hills and rugged cliffs, Lake Nyos of west central Africa looks like the perfect fishing hole or placid place for a waterfront picnic spot.

Oh, no!
Lake Nyos's calm surface hides a deadly secret. Formed in the crater of a volcano, the lake sits above a pocket of molten rock that percolates carbon dioxide into the water. The gas builds up in the lake's depths over time until it's released in a silent limnic eruption that turns the water from blue to brown and floods the countryside in suffocating carbon dioxide. One such eruption in 1986 killed nearly 2,000 people in nearby towns and villages. Today, a fountain at the lake's center pumps gassy water from the bottom to relieve carbon dioxide buildup. Scientists are unsure if this device will prevent another lethal eruption.

OH, No!

DEVIL'S POOL
(ZAMBIA, AFRICA)

Oh, wow!
The most spectacular swimming spot in the world is just knee deep and a bit brisk for itty-bitty bathing suits, but people don't leap into the appropriately named Devil's Pool for a soothing soak. This naturally formed tub sits right at the edge of Victoria Falls, offering a front-row seat to a 300-foot (91-m) plunge and the rainbow-colored plume created by the world's largest waterfall. Daring swimmers dive in and belly up to the edge for the ultimate photo op. Would you?

Oh, no!
A slippery rock ledge prevents people from being swept over the falls during the region's dry months (from May to October). The rest of the year, the fall's flow is much too powerful for a dip in Devil's Pool. That doesn't stop people from slipping into the water and cascading over the ledge to their doom.

CAVE OF THE CRYSTALS
(CHIHUAHUA, MEXICO)

Oh, wow!
Crisscrossed with crystals larger than power poles—the largest is 39 feet (12 m) long and 13 feet (4 m) around—this horseshoe-shaped cavern looks like Superman's Fortress of Solitude. The crystals formed over half a million years from mineral-rich water kept at intense temperatures by a molten-rock chamber below the cave, about a thousand feet (305 m) underground.

Oh, no!
Linger for longer than 15 minutes in the Cave of the Crystals and you may never leave. The magma below the cavern keeps the chamber at a constant 120 degrees Fahrenheit (49°C), almost as hot as the hottest spot on Earth. That extreme temperature combined with the high humidity leads to heat exhaustion and death (the cave has claimed at least one victim). Scientists must wear special cooling suits to study this beautiful, hostile environment.

TURN THE PAGE TO SEE THE DEADLIEST NATURAL WONDERS OF ALL!

MOUNT EVEREST
SAVAGE
SUMMIT

MOUNT EVEREST ISN'T JUST THE WORLD'S TALLEST MOUNTAIN. IT'S THE HIGHEST GRAVEYARD ON EARTH—AND HERE THE BODIES AREN'T BURIED. High in the Himalaya, nearly at the altitude flown by passenger planes, more than 150 corpses litter the rugged landscape. They sit or sprawl where they died, some of the bodies decades old, mummified and preserved by the harsh sun and freezing wind in an environment as dry as a desert. Their brightly colored jackets, pants, and boots stand out from the snow. Climbers working their way to the summit can't miss them.

Removing the bodies is much too dangerous; people who tried to recover Everest's victims have become victims themselves. And so the sky-high graveyard grows each year as more climbers go up but never come down. Here's what makes the "top of the world" so terrifyingly deadly ...

STORM TOSSED

Everest's peak juts into the jet stream—the river of air raging through Earth's stratosphere—and that makes for unpredictable weather. Although climbing teams take every precaution and schedule summit attempts in the mildest times of year, wild storms can roll in with little warning. Extreme winds up to 200 miles an hour (322 km/h) and blizzard conditions magnify the dangers and confusion of high-altitude climbing. Fifteen climbers lost their lives in a sudden storm in 1996, Everest's deadliest year.

BITING COLD

Even if Everest doesn't take your life, it can still leave its mark. The average temperature at the top is minus 17 degrees Fahrenheit (-27°C), but that can drop to nearly minus 100 degrees Fahrenheit (-73°C) in high winds. Any exposed skin suffers from frostbite, an agonizing condition in which blood drains from fingers and faces to preserve the body's core temperature. If heat and blood flow isn't restored fast enough, the tissue turns black and dies, resulting in amputation when—and if—the climber returns to civilization.

NO TURNING **BACK**

An expedition up Everest costs more than most luxury cars, but that doesn't stop hundreds of adventurers from trying to summit the mountain each year. Only about a hundred people reached the top in 1990; 20 years later, more than 500 climbers clambered to the summit. Most climbers lack experience in high-altitude climbing. They become caught in the grip of "summit fever," the drive to keep climbing despite worsening weather or lacking the strength to return. Crowded conditions on the mountain result in more deaths. Nearly 250 people have died climbing Everest since the first attempts were made in 1921. Many of the dead remain where they fell, grim monuments to the "Death Zone."

ON **EDGE**

Deep crevasses—or chasms in the ice—crisscross the route up Everest. Disoriented or careless climbers can tumble to their deaths.

THIN **AIR**

Most of Everest's victims don't perish from accidental falls or other climbing mishaps. Instead, they're done in by the Death Zone, a region above 26,000 feet (8,000 m) where the air holds only a third of the oxygen we inhale at sea level. Even with the help of bottled air, climbers can become befuddled, dizzy, and tired at this altitude—and yet they still must scramble up another 3,000 feet (900 m) to reach the summit. Exhausted and confused, some oxygen-starved climbers just sit down and give up. The Death Zone's deadly conditions make rescue nearly impossible.

TIM
THE GRIM REAPER'S
FATAL FACTS

Roughly 1 out of every 100 climbers who try to climb Everest die, but it's not the deadliest or most difficult mountain in the world. Nearby Annapurna peak and Pakistan's K2 claim more climbers' lives per summit attempt.

HOUSE OF

Six HIDDEN DANGERS at home (and how to fix them) ...

BAD **GAS**

Carbon monoxide (CO) is known as the silent killer for a scary reason: It's an odorless, tasteless, colorless gas that kills about 500 people in the United States each year. CO is created as exhaust from gas-burning space heaters, stoves, and water heaters, as well as fireplaces and wood-burning stoves. Clogged chimneys and bad ventilation can lead to a buildup of the gas, which causes flulike symptoms and eventually death.

MAKING IT SAFE: Make sure the house has a carbon monoxide detector, which warns when CO reaches dangerous levels in the house.

FUNKY **FUNGUS**

Mold grows on more than just shower tiles and that slice of cheese pizza you forgot in the fridge. This microscopic fungus sprouts anywhere with air and moisture. That includes any part of your house that's damp for at least two days (such as the soggy ceiling under a roof leak or the wall of a bathroom shower). Some molds can lead to serious health problems, including lung infections, asthma attacks, and burning eyes.

MAKING IT SAFE: Your parents can wipe away many molds with dishwashing soap, but major mold problems require the removal and replacement of the affected walls or carpets (but only after the source of the moisture—such as a leaky roof or wall—is fixed first).

KITCHEN **NIGHTMARE**

The most germ-ridden room in your house just happens to be where you make all your sandwiches. Studies show your toilet seat is actually cleaner than your kitchen counter! Blame the dish sponge and cutting board. Both have damp nooks that nourish bad bacteria—including sickening salmonella and E. coli—picked up from raw meat prepared nearby. These germs can trigger vomiting and diarrhea (or worse) if they get into your guts.

MAKING IT SAFE: Don't clean the countertops with that icky dish sponge (unless you zap it in the microwave for 30 seconds first). Keep raw beef, chicken, or seafood away from other foods, and dedicate a cutting board to preparing only those food items.

HORRORS

BATHROOM OF **DOOM**

According to the Centers for Disease Control and Prevention, your bathroom is the most dangerous room in the house. More than 200,000 Americans take a trip to the hospital each year because of bathroom accidents. Your slippery bathtub or shower is mostly to blame. Two-thirds of all emergency room visits result from falls in the tub or shower, particularly among people 15 to 24 years old.

MAKING IT SAFE: Slow down when you're done with your rubber ducky! Most falls happen after the shower is wet, when people are drying off and stepping out. If you're particularly accident prone, ask your parents to install a safety bar on the wall.

OUTLET **OVERLOAD**

It's tempting to plug your game console, TV, stereo system, computer, phone charger, tablet charger, and a power strip into that convenient power outlet under your desk. Don't do it! Overloaded outlets generate heat that gradually wears out wiring in your wall, which can ignite a fire. Overloaded outlets are responsible for more than 5,000 fires each year in the United States.

MAKING IT SAFE: Never connect multiple power strips to other power strips (a dangerous practice known as daisy-chaining), and make sure you have a smoke detector in your bedroom.

TOXIC **WASTE**

Pesticides, household cleaners, solvents, motor oil, paint—poisons are a necessary evil in home maintenance. They can also be deadly if they fall into young hands.

MAKING IT SAFE: Make sure your parents keep all these chemicals under lock and key, safely out of reach in a garage or basement cabinet. Bug-killing pesticides are especially lethal, so step outside when they're being sprayed or applied, and wash your hands with lots of soap if you accidentally touch any.

Enter the fallout zone of the
world's worst nuclear disaster ...

Wastela

YOU WON'T FIND ANY LINES FOR THE FERRIS WHEEL OR BUMPER CARS AT THE AMUSEMENT PARK IN THE CENTER OF PRIPYAT, UKRAINE. In fact, you won't find anyone at all. The rides haven't stirred in decades. The entire town is empty except for the wild animals that wander into stores and apartment buildings.

Pripyat was built to house workers for the nearby Chernobyl Nuclear Power Plant, site of the world's worst atomic disaster. When one of the plant's reactors exploded in 1986, it unleashed a cloud of radiation. The town's 50,000 residents scrambled to evacuate in just four hours, leaving behind furniture, food, toys, and other belongings.

Why the mad dash? The type of radiation created by nuclear power plants is deadly to humans, causing death through direct exposure to high amounts. Smaller doses farther from the site of the accident can cause deadly cancers and other life-threatening diseases. Chernobyl's cloud of radiation grew so vast that it blanketed parts of Europe. And while death tolls for the disaster are controversial and debatable, one estimate puts the number at nearly a million.

Today, radiation levels are still dangerously high in Pripyat, which remains a ghost town. The amusement park sits empty and eerily silent, a place frozen in time.

nd

MORE HOT SPOTS

HANFORD SITE

During the Cold War—a period of intense superpower rivalry between the United States and the former Soviet Union—this facility in Washington, U.S.A., manufactured plutonium for America's nuclear weapons. Today, it holds more than two-thirds of the country's deadly radioactive waste.

FUKUSHIMA

An earthquake and subsequent tsunami in 2011 rocked this seaside nuclear power plant in Japan, triggering the worst nuclear accident since Chernobyl. Half of the plant's six reactors were damaged, leaking radiation into the surrounding countryside and nearby ocean. Scientists are still determining the extent of the radiation damage.

BIKINI ATOLL

To test its nuclear arsenal, the United States military detonated a hydrogen bomb on this tiny stretch of coral and limestone in the Marshall Islands in 1954. The fallout from the bomb turned this Pacific paradise into a radioactive wasteland that remains dangerous today.

FATAL DESTINATIONS

TAKE A TERRIFYING TRIP TO THESE FATAL ATTRACTIONS ...

ROYAL ARMOURIES MUSEUM

LEEDS, ENGLAND

Look at (but don't touch) some 70,000 wares of war—from the gleaming swords of medieval kings to the quick-draw pistols of Wild West gunslingers—at this collection of history's most fascinating arms and armor. Defense as well as offense is on display, including the world's largest example of animal armor, tailor-made for an elephant.

MUSEUM OF DEATH

HOLLYWOOD, CALIFORNIA, U.S.A.

Tour the world's largest collection of execution devices, autopsy instruments, body bags, and coffins of every size and shape at this museum devoted to the bitter end, located off a busy tourist drag in Tinseltown. The museum is open to all ages, although be warned that guests have fainted from fright.

152

FLORIDA MUSEUM OF NATURAL HISTORY

GAINESVILLE, FLORIDA, U.S.A.

Home of the International Shark Attack File—a database of deadly finned-fish encounters from all over the world—this museum offers terrifying details of real-life shark attacks along with reassuring statistics showing just how rare these attacks really are. If the exhibit on the giant megalodon shark scares you out of the water, remind yourself that this bus-size predator has been extinct for 1.5 million years.

MUMMY MUSEUM OF GUANAJUATO

GUANAJUATO, MEXICO

Tourists can stare death in the face—actually, the well-preserved faces of 111 mummified bodies—at this popular museum in central Mexico. But unlike the mummies of ancient Egypt and other parts of the world, Guanajuato's deceased were preserved by accident rather than design. The bodies of men, women, and children (including the world's smallest mummy) were removed from their crypts from 1865 through 1958 when relatives could no longer afford a grave tax. Today, they're on display.

ALNWICK CASTLE POISON GARDEN

NORTHUMBERLAND, ENGLAND

Built in the 11th century, this sprawling castle in northern England is well known as the backdrop for Hogwarts in the first two Harry Potter movies, but it contains a secret garden that could stock a semester's worth of Severus Snape's potions. Called the Poison Garden, this popular attraction was planted by the Duchess of Northumberland, who figured that children would be spellbound by foxgloves, belladonnas, and other forbidden flora. Guided tours are led from a safe distance. Castle gardeners wear gloves, handling each poisonous plant with care.

TIM
THE GRIM REAPER'S
FATAL FACTS

According to the International Shark Attack File's statistics, you're more likely to perish in a collapsing sand-hole accident at the beach than in the jaws of a hungry shark. Which brings up the obvious point: Don't play in sand holes and tunnels at the beach! (But it's probably a good idea to stay away from sharks anyway.)

THREE
DEADLY
DRIVES

KARAKORAM HIGHWAY (PAKISTAN)

Car sickness is the least of a long list of concerns drivers face when they climb this stomach-churning mountain highway often rocked by landslides and socked in by rainy weather. The Karakoram Highway links China and Pakistan at an altitude of more than 15,000 feet (4,572 m), becoming an unpaved tract of loose gravel on the Pakistan side. Driving through this popular-with-travelers pass is treacherous enough; building it was even more dangerous. Nearly 900 workers died in landslides and other accidents.

TAROKO GORGE ROAD (TAIWAN)

With views to die for—sometimes literally—this busy mountain highway bores through the mountains of central Taiwan. Vistas of waterfalls and the river far below are a distraction for drivers contending with sharp turns and narrow sections they must share with tour buses, motorcycles, and even pedestrians. Heavy rains from hurricanes (called typhoons in this part of the world) can also loosen the rock walls and cause landslides.

NORTH YUNGAS ROAD (BOLIVIA)

Speeding trucks and packed buses attempt to pass each other with no space to spare on this skinny mountainside road that twists 38 miles (61 km) through treacherous terrain. As many as 300 drivers and passengers plummet to their dooms each year, earning this highway the name "Death Road" and the title for world's deadliest byway. Despite the danger, this highway is all the rage with thrill-seeking bicyclists who don't mind the lack of guardrails or trucks whizzing by inches from their handlebars.

KILLER Commutes

SUDDEN DEATH

RUN FOR YOUR LIFE!

DANGER ZONE

RISKY BUSINESS

North Yungas Road

Mount Everest

Chernobyl

Slot Canyons

Australian Outback

Peat Bogs

KILL-O-METER

DEAD ENDS

TIM
THE GRIM REAPER
RANKS LETHAL LOCATIONS

155

CHAPTER **8**

Life
After Deadly

CONGRATULATIONS, FEARLESS READER—you've nearly reached the end of your

treacherous trek through tales of toxins, teeth, terrifying history, and nature run amok. You're a survivor! By now, you're probably ready for a vacation from all the apocalyptic topics. Escape into this chapter full of fun games and pop quizzes that will ease you from danger mode into your safe, secure life. You might even impress your friends and family with your survival skills in the process!

SHARK ESCAPE

Millions of people play in the ocean every year; fewer than a hundred get bitten by a shark. But while encounters with these fierce fish are rare, an attack can literally cost you an arm and a leg. Check your odds at dodging a shark's jaws by taking our shark-attack final exam ...

1

What's the best time to swim if you want to avoid sharks?
A) Early in the morning
B) Middle of the day
C) At dusk
D) None of the above

2

True or False?
Sharks are more likely to attack swimmers who swim in a group.

3

Which places should you avoid to decrease your likelihood of a shark encounter?
A) Near river mouths
B) Areas between sandbars
C) Near fishermen and diving seabirds
D) All of the above

WHALE SHARK

BASKING SHARK

TIGER SHARK

4
Which of the sharks in these photos has been known to attack humans?
A) Whale Shark
B) Basking Shark
C) Tiger Shark
D) All of the above

5
True or False?
Sharks live only in salt water.

6
A shark is more likely to attack you if ...
A) ... you're bleeding.
B) ... you're wearing shiny objects.
C) ... you're sitting on a surfboard.
D) All of the above

7
If an aggressive shark approaches you, you should ...
A) ... splash the water to scare it off.
B) ... punch it in the eyes, nose, or gills.
C) ... pretend you're dead.
D) All of the above

Answers: 1 : B. Most shark attacks happen during the dawn or twilight hours. 2 : False. Sharks tend to target lone swimmers or stragglers from a group. 3 : D. Avoid all these areas—as well as steep drop-offs—if you don't want to end up as shark bait. 4 : C. Only the tiger shark has attacked humans. Whale sharks (A) and basking sharks (B) only look like they'd sample a swimmer. 5 : False. Deadly bull sharks can live in both the ocean and freshwater streams and rivers. A shark killed an 11-year-old boy and a man who tried to rescue him in an infamous 1916 attack in Matawan Creek, New Jersey, U.S.A., 15 miles (25 km) from the ocean. 6 : D. Sharks have attacked swimmers that met all of these qualifications. Leave the water at once if you're bleeding. Don't wear shiny objects or jewelry that a shark might mistake for fish scales. And limit your surfing to the times of the year when large sharks aren't in the area. 7 : B. Your best defense in a shark attack is a strong offense. Strike the shark in its most sensitive areas. Splashing and playing dead will only attract the curiosity of an aggressive shark.

MYSTERY MOUTHS

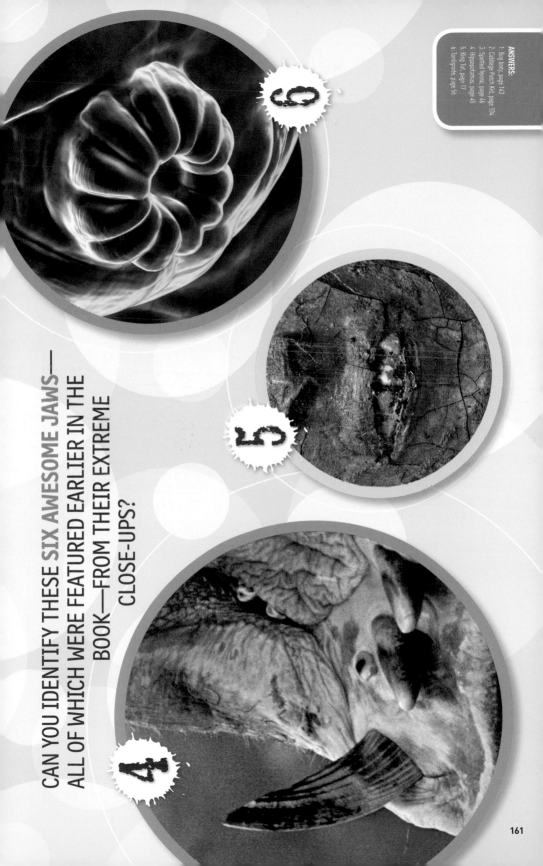

CAN YOU IDENTIFY THESE SIX AWESOME JAWS—ALL OF WHICH WERE FEATURED EARLIER IN THE BOOK—FROM THEIR EXTREME CLOSE-UPS?

ANSWERS:
1. Bug body, page 143
2. Cabbage Patch Kid, page 194
3. Spotted hyena, page 46
4. Hippopotamus, page 45
5. King Tut, page 17
6. Tardigrade, page 56

DODGING DISASTER

When the sky rumbles or the ground trembles or the wind starts to wail, it's time to put your survival plan into action. Check this test to see whether you will weather the storm or become just another statistic ...

1

When is it safe to head outside after a thunderstorm?
A) As soon as you don't see any lightning flashes
B) At least 30 minutes after the last thunderclap
C) The next morning
D) None of the above

True or False?
Calm weather during a hurricane signals that the storm has passed. All is clear!

2

If you're inside during a storm, you should avoid using ...
A) ... a landline phone.
B) ... water faucets or the shower.
C) ... a swimming pool.
D) All of the above

3

Wait for authorities or professional weather forecasters to report that a storm has passed. 4: D. Any one of these cataclysmic events could trigger a tsunami. 5: True. Rip currents aren't very wide, so you can usually escape them quickly if you just swim parallel to the beach. Swimming against them will only tire you out. 6: B. If you can't make it to a shelter in a tornado, the safest place is a windowless room—such as a closet, bathroom, or hallway—deep in your house.

4

Which of these events can cause a tsunami?

A) Earthquakes
B) Volcanic eruptions
C) Asteroid impacts
D) All of the above

DANGER

DANGEROUS RIP

SWIMMING PROHIBITED

5

True or False?

If you're caught in a rip current, swim parallel (or along) the beach rather than directly to shore.

6

If you're at home when a tornado strikes and you don't have a storm shelter beneath your house …

A) … run to the window so you can keep an eye on the twister.
B) … head to the nearest room without any windows.
C) … leave the house and climb into the nearest car.
D) None of the above

Answers: 1 : B. According to the 30/30 rule of lightning safety, you should head indoors in a storm if you can't count to 30 between a lightning flash and its thunderclap, and you should stay indoors for at least 30 minutes after hearing the last thunderclap. **2 : D.** If lightning strikes your house, it can zap you through the water pipes or the phone line. And definitely stay out of your swimming pool! **3: False. 4** Which one: **5:** True. **6: B.** Run to the nearest room without windows—and don't waste time opening windows to equalize pressure, which is a myth.

GEAR UP!

MATCH THE TOOL ON THE LEFT WITH THE DANGER IT DEALS WITH ON THE RIGHT ...

2

3

4

5

ANSWERS: 1: C. Skiers, snowshoers, and other alpine explorers should always wear an avalanche transceiver: a small tracking beacon that will lead rescuers to their location if they're buried in an avalanche. 2: D. If your house is in the path of a tornado, seek shelter in the basement or a first-floor hallway. 3: E. Seek the high ground if you're in an area prone to flash flooding (such as a gully or river basin) during periods of heavy rain. 4: B. A lightning rod is a metal object mounted on the top of a tall structure and wired to the ground. It provides a path for lightning to follow to the ground rather than passing through the building and potentially starting a fire or hurting the people inside. 5: A. Your best bet for surviving a volcanic eruption is to evacuate well before the volcano blows its top. Geologists who study these magma-spewing mountains wear special fire proximity suits insulated to protect against temperatures up to 2,000 degrees Fahrenheit (1093°C).

E

D

C

B

A

STRIKE ZONE

Unless you visit a reptile zoo, work as an exterminator, or live in Australia, chances are you'll never encounter a deadly venomous creature. But, hey—it always pays to be prepared. Check your skill at avoiding stinging sensations in this final exam of *That's Deadly!*

1

You can tell a venomous snake from a nonvenomous one because it has ...
A) ... a triangular head instead of a rounded one.
B) ... slits for pupils in its eyes instead of round pupils.
C) ... pits between its eyes and its nostrils.
D) All of the above

2

True or False?
Poisonous animals inject toxins through their fangs or stingers.

3

What's the best way to protect yourself from jellyfish stings?
A) Smear on extra sunscreen.
B) Wear panty hose over your exposed skin.
C) Don't enter water any deeper than your waist.
D) None of the above

running until the chase. Running through bushes or shrubbery will help throw off the swarm, as well. 5: True. The vivid colors of poisonous animals warn predators not to eat them. 6: A. Remember this rhyme to tell the difference between a harmless milk snake and a deadly coral snake: "Red
on yellow kills a fellow. Red on black is a friend of Jack." The rhyme's colorful words refer to the order of the snake's stripes. If the snake has yellow stripes
next to the red ones, keep your distance! [Again! you shouldn't mess with a snake regardless of its color.]

If you disturb a hive of bees, immediately ...
A) ... dive into the nearest body of water.
B) ... smack the bees as they swoop in to sting you.
C) ... stretch your jacket or shirt so it covers your head and arms.
D) None of the above

5

True or False?
Poisonous animals tend to be brightly colored.

6

You can tell a coral snake—North America's deadliest serpent— from its harmless mimics by this color scheme:
A) Yellow stripes next to red ones
B) Black stripes next to red ones
C) Green stripes next to purple ones
D) Solid black color

Komodo dragon

Tiger snake

POiSONOUS
OR Venomous?

Guess the type of toxin in each of these potentially lethal creatures
(for a refresher on poisons versus venoms, see page 118) ...

Black mamba

Lionfish

Deathstalker scorpion

Poison dart frog

Slow loris

Whip spider

Answers: Komodo dragon: Venomous. Researchers only recently learned that these large lizards have venomous mouths just like snakes. **Tiger snake:** Both. The snake has a venomous bite and poisonous skin. **Death-stalker scorpion:** Venomous. Venom is injected through its tail stinger. **Poison dart frog:** Poisonous, of course. **Slow loris:** Tricky. This Ewok-like primate of Southeast Asia secretes poison from its armpits, but then applies the poison to its teeth to deliver a toxic bite similar to a venomous animal. **Whip spider:** Neither. If it looks could kill, this scorpion cousin could scare you to death. Fear not! The harmless whip spider lacks its relatives' stinger-tipped tail. **Lionfish:** Venomous. This invasive species injects venom from its needlelike fins. **Black mamba:** Venomous.

169

ULTIMATE DEATH MATCH

WHiCH LiFE-FORM iS THE MOST LETHAL?

TIGER

The biggest of the big cats, tigers are also the deadliest, responsible for the most attacks on humans.

AFRICAN BUFFALO

This bulletproof African bull bears a grudge against anything—or anyone—that threatens the herd.

LIONFISH

Few sea creatures can survive an encounter with this venomous invasive species.

TIGER SHARK

It's called the "garbage can of the sea" for its insatiable appetite, but can the tiger shark trash the lionfish?

NILE CROCODILE

This massive African crocodilian kills up to 200 people a year.

HIPPOPOTAMUS

Don't let its cute looks fool you. Hippos are territorial terrors with a powerful bite.

TAIPAN

One strike from this Australian serpent packs enough venom to kill more than a hundred humans.

MOSQUITO

Slurp, slurp, slurp! This bloodthirsty bug doesn't drink to your health.

AFRICAN BUFFALO

Not even a tiger or a whole pride of lions can beat an African buffalo in a bad mood.

TIGER SHARK

Sharks are one of the few predators that can eat lionfish. But can it handle a mad cow?

NILE CROCODILE

Nile crocs have survived since the days of the dinosaurs. They're not about to give up now.

MOSQUITO

Swat one of these disease-spreading insects and another takes its place.

THE END IS NEAR, BUT TIM THE GRIM REAPER ISN'T DONE DEALING WITH DEADLY TOPICS JUST YET! Your scary skeletal host has scoured the seas, swamps, forests, and even your backyard to round up some of the killer creatures covered in this book for a tournament of terror. This isn't simply a contest to see which animal has the biggest jaws or the most venomous sting; it's a showdown to measure the capacity to kill and avoid being killed. Though these animals aren't actually likely to meet in the wild, only one will reign as king or queen of all things lethal! Don't agree with Tim's choices? Draw your own tournament bracket on a piece of paper and determine your own terminal titan!

TIGER SHARK
Smelling blood in the water, the shark circles for the kill.

MOSQUITO
This bug doesn't float like a butterfly or sting like a bee, but it's certainly more deadly.

AND THE MOST LETHAL LiFE-FORM iS ...
THE MOSQUiTO!

Buzzing from person to person in certain parts of the world, this bloodsucking bug spreads malaria, dengue fever, and other diseases that kill more people per year than all the other animals in this competition. So the next time you smack a mosquito that's nibbling on your neck, consider this: **YOU WERE JUST BITTEN BY THE WORLD'S DEADLIEST ANIMAL!**

Famous LAST WORDS

The final thoughts of famous people...

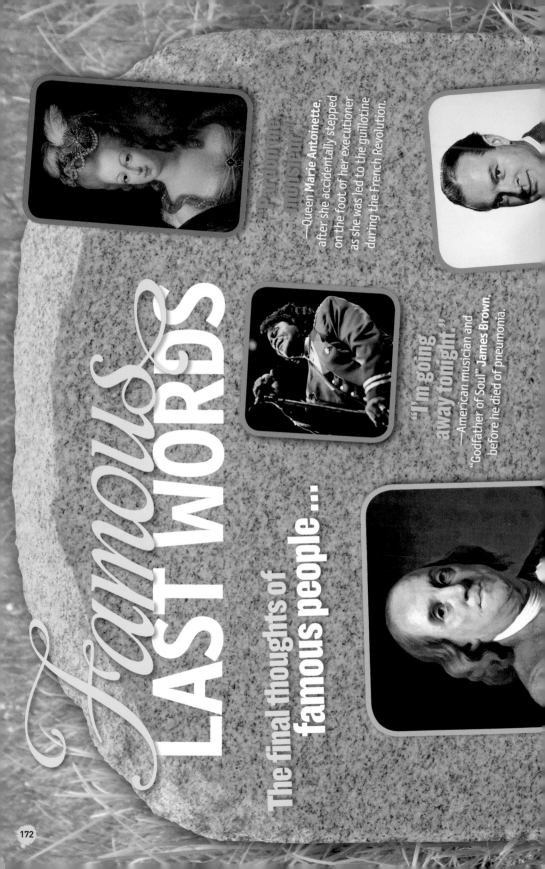

"Pardon me, monsieur."
—Queen Marie Antoinette, after she accidentally stepped on the foot of her executioner as she was led to the guillotine during the French Revolution.

"I'm going away tonight."
—American musician and "Godfather of Soul" James Brown, before he died of pneumonia.

"Surprise me."

—Comedian and actor **Bob Hope** from his deathbed, when his wife asked him where he wanted to be buried.

"All good things must come to an end, so I hope you enjoyed the book. I'll see you again ... someday. *Muahahaha!*"

—**TIM THE GRIM REAPER**, host of *That's Deadly!*

"I only regret that I have but one life to give for my country."

—American spy **Nathan Hale**, right before he was hanged by the British during the Revolutionary War.

"A dying man can do nothing easily."

—Founding Father **Benjamin Franklin** before he perished in his deathbed.

You will no longer live in Arcturus!

—Allegedly the last words of **Nostradamus**, the French seer who published prophecies of the future.

"Last words are for fools who haven't said enough."

—German philosopher and revolutionary **Karl Marx**, just before he died of illness in 1883.

INDEX

Dedicated to Sean "Seanbaby" Reiley,
whose feet, fists, and wit are registered
as deadly weapons. —CB

Staff for This Book
Becky Baines, *Senior Editor*
Julide Dengel, *Art Director*
Dawn McFadin, *Designer*
Margaret Sidlosky, *Photo Editor*
Paige Towler, *Editorial Assistant*
Sanjida Rashid and Rachel Kenny,
    Design Production Assistants
Colm McKeveny, *Rights Clearance Specialist*
Grace Hill, *Managing Editor*
Michael O'Connor, *Production Editor*
Lewis R. Bassford, *Production Manager*
Rachel Faulise, *Manager, Production Services*
Susan Borke, *Legal and Business Affairs*

Published by the National Geographic Society
Gary E. Knell, *President and CEO*
John M. Fahey, *Chairman of the Board*
Melina Gerosa Bellows, *Chief Education Officer*
Declan Moore, *Chief Media Officer*
Hector Sierra, *Senior Vice President and General
    Manager, Book Division*

Senior Management Team, Kids Publishing and Media
Nancy Laties Feresten, *Senior Vice President*
Jennifer Emmett, *Vice President, Editorial
    Director, Kids Books*
Julie Vosburgh Agnone, *Vice President, Editorial
    Operations*
Rachel Buchholz, *Editor and Vice President,
    NG Kids magazine*
Michelle Sullivan, *Vice President, Kids Digital*
Eva Absher-Schantz, *Design Director*
Jay Sumner, *Photo Director*
Hannah August, *Marketing Director*
R. Gary Colbert, *Production Director*

Digital
Anne McCormack, *Director*
Laura Goertzel, Sara Zeglin, *Producers*
Emma Rigney, *Creative Producer*
Bianca Bowman, *Assistant Producer*
Natalie Jones, *Senior Product Manager*

The National Geographic Society is one of the world's largest nonprofit scientific and educational organizations. Founded in 1888 to "increase and diffuse geographic knowledge," the Society's mission is to inspire people to care about the planet. It reaches more than 400 million people worldwide each month through its official journal, *National Geographic*, and other magazines; National Geographic Channel; television documentaries; music; radio; films; books; DVDs; maps; exhibitions; live events; school publishing programs; interactive media; and merchandise. National Geographic has funded more than 10,000 scientific research, conservation, and exploration projects and supports an education program promoting geographic literacy.

For more information, please visit nationalgeographic.com, call 1-800-NGS LINE (647-5463), or write to the following address:

National Geographic Society
1145 17th Street N.W.
Washington, D.C. 20036-4688 U.S.A.

Visit us online at nationalgeographic.com/books

For librarians and teachers: ngchildrensbooks.org

More for kids from National Geographic: kids.nationalgeographic.com

For information about special discounts for bulk purchases, please contact National Geographic Books Special Sales: ngspecsales@ngs.org

For rights or permissions inquiries, please contact National Geographic Books Subsidiary Rights: ngbookrights@ngs.org

Paperback ISBN: 978-1-4263-2078-1
Reinforced library binding ISBN: 978-1-4263-2079-8

Printed in Hong Kong
15/THK/1